A Special Mother is Born

A Special Mother is Born

Parents share how God called them to the extraordinary
vocation of parenting a special needs child

LETICIA VELASQUEZ

Including Stories from Barbara Curtis, former Senator
Rick Santorum, Lisa Barker, and Dr. Gerard Nadal
Foreword by Mother Mary Agnes Donovan, SV

WestBow
PRESS
A DIVISION OF THOMAS NELSON

WestBow Press books may be ordered through booksellers or by contacting:

WestBow Press
A Division of Thomas Nelson
1663 Liberty Drive
Bloomington, IN 47403
www.westbowpress.com
1-(866) 928-1240

ISBN: 978-1-4497-2416-0 (sc)
ISBN: 978-1-4497-2417-7 (e)

Library of Congress Control Number: 2011917177

Printed in the United States of America

WestBow Press rev. date: 10/18/2011

Endorsements for "A Special Mother is Born"

As the father of a child with trisomy 21, I am delighted that A *Special Mother is Born* is highlighting the gift that children with Down syndrome are to those mothers (and fathers) who are blessed with them. In a barbaric age that routinely kills these children in the womb, such a book is needed as a beacon of light and hope in a darkened world.

Joseph Pearce, author of The Quest for Shakespeare *and EWTN Show Host*

In this wonderful book, Leticia Velasquez has given her readers a gift of parental faith, wrapped in encouragement and adorned with a bow of hope. Through my vocation as well as membership in the Knights of Columbus, I have had the privilege of spending time with many of these bright and beautiful children of God. It is not about special needs but special blessings – those we give and those we receive. I highly commend this book. If you are a mom, dad, uncle, aunt, grandma or grandpa – you may want to keep some tissues handy. These stories will tug on your heart and touch your soul.

Randy Sly, Associate Editor Catholic Online - International Edition

This book is not just for families of special needs children. Not by a long shot. There is truth, love and joy in these pages for everyone to draw on. We are all disabled; all needing help and all falling short in one way or another.

During my years as a writer, I've interviewed many parents of special needs children and come to understand that special children bring special blessings to their families. Again and again I've seen the transforming power of these children. While mental and physical abilities below par are seen as a handicap, the world often forgets to weight the power of a loving heart and innocent soul. In such an equation, which of us is really handicapped?

Today, when so many end the life of an unborn child with abnormal chromosomes, my heart breaks for them. They choose to turn down a blessing that would have expanded their hearts and souls and better prepared them for Heaven. These stories will touch your heart so that you will come away thinking: they (or we) are so blessed!

Patti Maguire Armstrong, Catholic Speaker and author, whose
articles and books can be found at www.RaisingCatholicKids.com

If we are to triumph in the war against the culture of death, we must build up our arsenals of beauty and hope. That's exactly what *A Special Mother is Born* does. The stories here are powerful in their potential to dispel fear and enable even the heaviest heart to soar.

Sherry Boas, special needs adoptive mother and author of a trilogy of novels
revolving around a character with Down Syndrome: Until Lily, Wherever
Lily Goes *and* Life Entwined with Lily's, *available at LilyTrilogy.com.*

Leticia Velasquez has compiled a tremendous resource for families with *A Special Mother is Born*. This book is a must-read not only for parents of special needs children, but for anyone who knows and loves a child who faces unique challenges in life. *A Special Mother is Born* shares the insights, experiences and personal stories of families who have recognized the true gift of life and been blessed by their lives with special needs children.

Lisa M. Hendey,
author of The Handbook for Catholic Moms

Story by true story, the parents of *A Special Mother is Born* echo the poignant and dramatic truth of the Prophet Isaiah's words, "... *and a little child shall lead them (Isa 11: 6)."* Come read 33 real-life accounts of parents of children with special needs. This book offers straight talk about the gritty and redeeming "soul" work of parenting as it radiates unvarnished encouragement for anyone facing similar challenges. Filled with moments of faith and frustration, turmoil and transcendence, these Moms and Dads --and their kids!-- will awaken your heart to the kaleidoscope of life's real joys, and the healing power of love. Leticia Velasquez has compiled a compelling collection of stories and social commentary that shines light on the beauty and dignity of every human person.

Pat Gohn, writer, catechist, and host of the Among Women podcast.

I pray that this book reaches all parents who help their children carry such huge crosses. I was deeply touched and honored to have my daughter's story included.

Lisa "Jelly Mom" Barker, author, columnist and administrator of the Catholic Mom Community

A Special Mother is Born is a major opportunity to learn about mothers of children with special needs -- don't miss it!

Florence Malone, Ed.D. Professor Emerita, City University of New York

The sincerity, frankness, and, ultimately, grace-filled joy of these essays by parents with special needs children will speak to every heart in that they touch on every aspect of the experience. Readers facing the news that they are expecting a special needs child will find honest echoes to their own range of emotions and thoughts. Families living with or having lived with a special needs child will nod, weep and even chuckle in grateful recognition. Those who have never had the experience will come away informed, uplifted and enlightened. And those who have harbored fear, resistance--or even worse--toward the reality of this aspect of human life will likely have their hearts and minds changed forever.

Josephine Nobisso, author of The Weight of a Mass,
Take It to the Queen, *and* Francis Woke Up Early

A Special Mother is Born provides timely information and experiences regarding the Down syndrome child. Reading Leticia's useful resource will open new doors while empowering parents, educators, legislators, who may have a whole new world of questions, to meet the varied needs of these exceptional children so they are not less valued according to society's beliefs and conventions.

This book contains up-to-date information for new parents, enabling them to become familiar with the latest resources which help children with Down syndrome to have meaningful, natural relationships and productive opportunities they deserve to develop confidence and talents - to be all they can. Many such kiddos attend college; have fulfilling careers and relationships, because research has increased a thousand fold over past years. *A Special Mother is Born* will help each of us to embrace these remarkable people whom God has entrusted to not only their natural parents but to all of us.

Barb Kralis, freelance journalist

Leticia Velasquez is a devoted and courageous mother, one of the rare breed who nurture their less-than-perfectly-predicted children and receive far more than could ever be expected in joyous reward. By publicizing her own family's treasure, she inspires others to embrace the fragile lives that will enrich their own.

Sister Marie-André Wilson, SCMC, Teens of Pro-Life Club, Academy of the Holy Family, Baltic, CT

A Special Mother is Born is a remarkable and joy-filled collection of inspirational families and their special needs children. The world has declared war on these children because they consider them a burden. However, Leticia Velasquez shows the world (through the many touching real-life stories from modern-day warriors within the Church Militant) that love always conquers. This book is an incredible motivational tool that brings about the essence and sanctity of life.

Ched Salasek, father of six, one of whom has Spina Bifida, and Family Advisor at the ADHS Office for Children with Special Health Care Needs.

In addition to beautiful and heartfelt accounts by parents of children with a variety of special needs and sincere accounts of their increased faith through their families' journeys, readers will be blessed by a wealth of information for all ages on related topics. Leticia Velasquez's collaborative gem, *A Special Mother is Born*, should have a place of honor on the shelves of ALL parents.

Christine Capolino, homeschooling Mom, writer, columnist for Mater et Magistra Magazine *and* Catholic Mom.com

Thank you for letting me be a part of such an incredibly special family that was brought together by the tremendous love of our children.

May all of these families be continually blessed by God in all ways!

Tamara Musella, contributor to A Special Mother is Born

"Who knew that a book about grief, loss, and a parents' worst nightmare be so shot through with life, encouragement--and humor?"

"Having had to say good-bye to a Partial trisomy 9 daughter at age 15 days, I will never forget the experience of helplessness before the suffering of your smallest, most precious, most exquisite little one. Leticia Velasquez has gathered together a moving selection of stories about how good people handled bad medical news; about the sudden surge of courage (usually segueing into a marathon) in the hearts of new parents faced with unexpected circumstances; and about the sanity-inducing reality of prayer."

"If someone you love (perhaps you?) is hurting over the severe physical impairments of a child, hand them these testimonies to the power of Christ's terrible, tender love. At a time when so many of these little persons are in the cross hairs of a culture of death, Velasquez has fought back with grace and elan. Read on and find out how."

Patrick Coffin, author and host of Catholic Answers Live

Contents

ENDORSEMENTS FOR "A SPECIAL MOTHER IS BORN"   v

FOREWORD   xv

INTRODUCTION   xvii

DEDICATION   xix

PART I
STORIES OF OUR BLESSINGS

Chapter 1: Joy and Peace in the Shadow of Death   3
by Lisa Barker

Chapter 2: Sadie's Story   8
by Eileen Haupt

Chapter 3: A Little Extra   13
by Barbara Curtis

Chapter 4: Peter's Story   17
by Mary Kellett

Chapter 5: Love Conquers All   22
by Tamara Musella

Chapter 6: St. Joseph and the Second Gift   28
by Janet M. Olesen

Chapter 7: A Faith Deepens Down Under   31
by Therese Royals

Chapter 8: The Quiet Joy   36
by Melissa Wiley

Chapter 9: A Change for the Better   40
by Shannon Rizzo

Chapter 10: Michael and Birgitta's Story   44
by Monica O'Brien

Chapter 11: The Path of Miracles   49
by Eileen Benthal

Chapter 12: The World Needs Wildflowers   55
by Mary Ellen Barrett

Chapter 13: Tony   58
by Mary von Schlegell

Chapter 14: Not My Plan   60
by Kathleen M. Basi

Chapter 15: The Hospital Visit   63
by Nancy Valko

Chapter 16: Two Years Worth Every Tear   66
by Rick Santorum

Chapter 17: A Doctor's Story   69
Dr. Judith Mascolo

Chapter 18: A Journey in Faith through RISEN   76
by Jane O'Friel, RN

Chapter 19: Choosing Life   80
by Christina Bogdan

Chapter 20: A Special Mother is Born   82
by Leticia Velasquez

Chapter 21: An Answer to Prayer   93
by Alicia Smith

Chapter 22: Our Grace-Filled Miracle   100
By Lissette Yellico

Chapter 23: Faith's Story   103
by Allison Gingras

Chapter 24: Simon's Story   109
by Gretchen Peters

Chapter 25: Answering the Call   114
by Kim Garvin

Chapter 26: Welcome to Rome   120
by Diane Grover

Chapter 27: Happy Birthday Eliza!   124
by Kimberlee Kadar-Kallen

Chapter 28: The Triumph of the Cross   127
by Helen Dilworth

Chapter 29: Gianna's Story   130
by Nicola Moore

Chapter 30: If I Had Known   136
by Margaret Mary Meyers

Chapter 31: An Autistic Child Shall Lead Them   142
by Gerard M. Nadal, Ph.D.

Chapter 32: The Woman in the Mirror   148
    by Heidi Hess-Saxton

Chapter 33: The Little Girl Who Lived a Novena   152
    by Colleen McGuire

Chapter 34: "Grace at the Heart of Grief"   160
    by Patrick Coffin

Chapter 35: Letter to a Special Needs Mother   168

PART II
SPECIAL MOTHERS PROCLAIM
THE GOSPEL OF LIFE

Chapter 36: When the war on our children began; the history of
            eugenic abortion   173

Chapter 37: Special Mothers Respond   186

APPENDIX I   199

APPENDIX II   209

ACKNOWLEDGEMENTS   225

EPILOGUE   227

Foreword

I first met Leticia Velasquez, appropriately, at an event of our community that we call LifeFest. It is a day of prayer and festivity held annually on the 4th of July to celebrate the gift of freedom and the gift of life. At LifeFest 2009, Leticia shared with me her inspiration to publish a collection of stories by mothers of children with special needs. As I looked out on the hundreds of children playing on the grounds of our convent that day, I also thought of all the children whose faces we will never see, because they do not conform to society's definition of a life worth living. Children diagnosed with a disability while still in the womb are being aborted at an alarmingly high rate. Their mothers often feel like they have no choice, after being abandoned by those closest to them and pressured by medical professionals who fail to see life as a gift. Every day, thousands of women are presented with an unexpected invitation to maternity and in order to give life to their child, must make nothing less than a heroic choice.

This book is a beautiful service to the culture of life. It will inspire and educate those who do not know the gift of children with special needs; and it will support, accompany and uphold those parents who have received an adverse pre-natal diagnosis or already love their own child with special needs. These testimonies of grace offer a magnificent witness to the beauty of motherhood and the power of children to bring joy to the lives of all whom they encounter. The call to special motherhood is a call to accept the gift of maternity in a way that a woman does not expect and does not feel equipped to embrace. As Leticia says of her own experience, she learned that God does not choose the equipped, bur rather He equips the chosen.

We read of the birth of Michael, whose condition paved the way for his parents to adopt another child with special needs, and of little Bella, who has defied all odds and survived past her second birthday, nourished by the love lavished upon her by her family. We also read the poem of an eighty-year-old mother whose forty-year-old son's only word has been Mama, and the story of Christina Anne, whose birth prompted her mother to discover an authentically Catholic approach to her vocation as a medical doctor. Page after page reveals the journeys of sacrificial love made by these mothers. And page after page tells of the ways God has blessed their choice by bringing them closer to Him through the lives of their children.

In his inaugural address after being elected, Pope Benedict told the world,

> "Each of us is the result of a thought of God. Each of us is willed, each of us is loved, each of us is necessary. There is nothing more beautiful than to be surprised by the Gospel, by the encounter with Christ. There is nothing more beautiful than to know Him and to speak to others of our friendship with Him."

The authors of these stories have allowed themselves to be surprised by the joy of the Gospel and the joy of love. They preach the *Gospel of Life* with their very lives and the lives of their children. In the midst of our expanding culture of death, they give words to the pain, suffering and ultimately the awe and wonder at seeing the face of God in the faces of their children. In the lives of these women, you will see living testaments to Jesus' promise in the Gospel of John where He tells His followers, "I came that they might have life and have it abundantly."

As you read these stories of life, pray for these women and all women chosen by God to be special mothers, that they may know the inestimable gift they have given the world by embracing their maternity.

Mother Agnes Mary Donovan, S.V.
Superior General
Sisters of Life

Introduction

"Christina has symptoms which are consistent with Down syndrome." The nurses were surrounding my gurney in the hallway outside the delivery room, when they uttered these fateful words. Words which hit my stomach like a sucker punch. I was frightened and overwhelmed, but I was not alone. Four months earlier, God had spoken to me about Christina in the depths of my heart. He told me that she had Down syndrome, and that she was a gift from His hand.

Even though I had four months to absorb these prophetic words, the reality of becoming a special needs mother hit me anew when Christina was born. Though I have given birth amid complications to three children, and have endured three miscarriages, this is, by far, the biggest challenge of my vocation as a mother.

Whether you are expecting a child or have already given birth to a child with special needs, the authors of this book have been where you are today. It is for you that we have compiled this collection of stories from mothers and fathers who have walked the same road.

The parents you are about to meet are ordinary men and women, most of whom never imagined themselves capable of raising a special needs child. However, when they received the call from Our Lord, they said "yes," even though, many seriously doubted their ability to cope with the unknown challenges of raising such a child. What they *did* know, through the eyes of faith, was that God doesn't always call the equipped; He equips the called. Their previous faith experiences and their love of Our Lord prepared them and gave them the courage to accept His holy will to give them a child with special needs without knowing precisely what challenges awaited them. In this way, they resemble Our Lady, whose fiat was one of complete surrender and trust in an unknown future, which would certainly hold both pain and glory. It was a trust that God's gifts are greater than we can imagine, and will lead us and our families to the glory of Heaven.

I wanted to share the spiritual beauty of these men and women, most of whom I know personally. They have impressed me with their joy, their wisdom and, above all, their calm assurance that "We know that all things work for good for those who love God, who are called according to his purpose" (Romans 8:28 NABRE). Some of the contributors to this book are great writers whose work has inspired me. All of them are exceptional examples of the vocation to special motherhood and fatherhood which is a call to deepen one's commitment to this vocation. It resembles the deepening of Blessed Mother Teresa's vocation as a sister, when she said "yes" to her famous "call within the call"; Jesus' request that she abandon the comfort of her convent in Calcutta to work in the slums with the poorest of the poor. God has called you to abandon the comfort of what parenthood means to you and tread the road less traveled and most often eschewed by society. To accept the vocation to special parenthood is most likely the most challenging thing you have ever done and no one should walk alone down this difficult road.

These mothers, fathers, and their amazing children were the inspiration for this book. I want you to know their stories, as they labor unnoticed within their homes, for we have many saints among us. When I shared my vision for this book, they enthusiastically told me they wanted to embrace you and offer you hope. Their stories, full of tears and triumph, joy and love, will accompany you on the blessed path of raising your special needs child. You are not alone.

Dedication

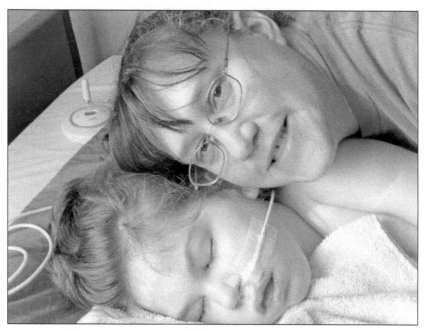

Lisa and Becca Boo Barker

We would like to dedicate this book to Rebecca Harrison-Barker, daughter of Lisa, who passed into eternity on July 11, 2010. Lisa told me she was offering her daughter's suffering for the success of this book, so we can thank Becca Boo for the grace brought into the hearts of those who read this book.

Ryan Barrett

We dedicate this book to Ryan Barrett, son of Mary Ellen, who left this world for the arms of Jesus while this book was being written. As a young man of 14, Ryan had his heart set on being a Franciscan Friar of the Renewal; his family has a close relationship with the Friars, and he was frequently found in their company, learning from them how to live for Christ. Now he is living with Christ in the company of the angels and saints.

Rita McGuire and her family

We want to dedicate this book to little Rita McGuire who lived a novena of nine days, and is now a saint in heaven.

Ryan, Rita, and Rebecca, we count on your prayers to open hearts and make this world a more welcoming place for God's wildflowers.

A Child Like No Other

OUR LADY BORE A CHILD LIKE NO OTHER

Mary Ellen Barrett has written that we who are mothering special needs children resemble Our Lady, for she, like us, had a Child like no other. Recently, I attended a Marian concert in our beautiful cathedral. I brought Christina, who can be a challenge in church; however the ancient motets and soaring hymns soon had her soundly asleep in my arms. I used the opportunity to ask Our Lady to explain what her Son has in common with special needs children. This is the result of that meditation.

Mary bore a Child like no other;

A Child who did not conform to society's expectations;

He was different from the others; He gazed upon Heaven when the rest could only see clouds.

He reminded them of their failings, their lack of charity, their shallowness, their impatience, and their rush to judgment.

His government tried to kill Him, and eventually succeeded.

He had to endure constant misunderstanding of what He was trying to communicate, and bore the frustration of those who misunderstood Him.

He was mocked and rejected, and at times, it seemed only His mother still stood by Him.

She felt the loneliness of seeing her Son rejected because He was different, yet she bore the pain patiently because she knew that it was for us, the 'least of these'. that He suffered and died.

Our Lady knew that our special children would, like her Son, be signs of contradiction in the world. Because of this, I believe that she asks her Son for extraordinary graces for them. These allow our children to see His face directly, free of the veil which clouds our vision, since most of our children are incapable of offending God.

She, being a Mother of mothers, knew that by mothering them, we would be offered rare but dazzling glimpses of the pure love of Jesus.

To sustain us when the darkness of this world threatens to overtake us, and to remind us that in Heaven our children will be healed of their infirmities and wholly appreciated for the gift they posses: unfathomable spiritual beauty.

They and we will be home.

Leticia Velasquez

Part 1

Stories of our blessings

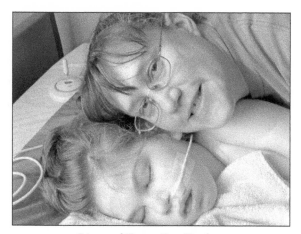

Lisa and Becca Boo Barker

Chapter 1

Joy and Peace in the Shadow of Death

by Lisa Barker

Boo was born with silvery hair and appeared as if she'd just been whisked away from the fairies. She was such a sweet and quiet newborn, early on sleeping well through the night. She'd make up for it by nursing all day long. She was a happy baby.

But by age two-and-a-half, she hadn't mastered many words, though she'd created a few of her own. She called me and every other woman "momma", she called her dad "bubba", every animal was a cat, and if she wanted to drink she asked for "dub way". We thought perhaps she was a little slow. So when we learned that she had a rare illness, Batten Disease, we were devastated. It doesn't allow for the cells in Boo's brain to output waste and in doing so kills off brain cells. There is no cure or treatment.

Suddenly the child who could balance expertly on a windowsill, a natural gymnast, was falling face first onto the floor and suffering seizures. She went from running and babbling and doing all the things most kiddos her age do, to becoming wheelchair bound within a year, barely able to crawl on the ground. We didn't have time to grieve, though it would hit us at any given time, like a train barreling down on us in slow motion.

I was there alone with her the day they told me my daughter's cerebellum was atrophied. "I can buy my baby a Happy Meal," I thought, blinking back the tears at a McDonald's afterward, "but I can't buy her a new cerebellum." Boo sat on the end of the slide, talking to me, filled with sheer enthusiasm about the colored slide and completely unaware that death was stalking her. "Hey, yeah!" she beamed, trying to draw me out of my sorrow. Little did she know that she had only about three to four years to live.

It's been five years since Boo's diagnosis. She's now eight-and-a-half years old (having given us a few more years of life than we had expected) and spends the majority of her time sleeping in a hospital bed in her room. She is completely oblivious to the suction machine and other medical equipment that surrounds her bed. Her experience is comfort. She lives in a little nest of blankets, and SpongeBob, her hero, plays 24/7 for her in case she awakens and no one is in the room at the moment. She sleeps on a mattress of memory foam and hears the sound of her large family bustling from room to room. Cats sleep on the end of her bed and warm her feet. She's completely bedridden and in a nearly incapacitated state. I like to think of her as an infant in the womb.

Before Boo could no longer communicate she used to talk to the angels. That's what I called it. She would suddenly fix her eyes on the ceiling and her face would totally light up and she'd start cooing and "talking" to things, beings we couldn't see. This euphoria would last for up to half an hour sometimes. It's rare that she speaks like this anymore, but Boo has made us aware that there's more to life than what mere mortal eyes can see.

I used to worry that I was a bad mom because I didn't pray and beg God for Boo's recovery. What kind of mother cares so little? Was my one or occasional request a sign of my lack of faith or my complete trust in God?

One day at Mass, Father said in his homily that he did not think he offered families false hope when he told them to pray for the healing of a sick loved one because God heals all people. Sometimes, though, he doesn't heal them on earth. He heals them in heaven. This is good enough for me. This belief is my one constant act of faith and hope, that God *will* heal Boo, though I believe He will choose to do so in Heaven.

A friend of mine confirmed this when she stood in for Boo at a healing Mass and the priest prayed over her. She said she could envision a little blonde girl running with absolute joy in a meadow and knew this was Boo in Heaven. And she thought, "But this isn't what we are praying for." But this is God's plan for my little girl. How can I deny God His plan and Boo's utter and ultimate happiness?

Because I have a mother's heart. This is my baby. I don't want to let go. I especially don't want to give her up to a cold unforgiving ground—a stark, empty, callous reality of death. But as Boo has progressed in her illness and as she becomes more infant-like, my peace with this has grown and I have entered into the experience of both the passion and death of our Lord through Boo. And, I have come to understand an elusive character in my faith journey: our Blessed Mother.

I've never been able to relate to Mary as my mother, at least not until Boo became ill. There is no prayer that spares us grief or that relieves us of that inescapable, inevitable moment of death. But through Jesus and Mary, with Jesus and Mary, in Jesus and Mary I can grieve without being consumed by the grief. I can stand at the foot of the Cross with Mary and grieve with her, mother to mother. I can watch my child die as she watched her child die. I can love and nurture, even through tears and pain.

Standing at the foot of the Cross I have found that I am in the most unexpected position to comfort others who suffer greatly. I can't take away their pain. I can't fix anything. But I *know* suffering and I know it isn't the end. My companions on the faith journey and I are free to weep.

In Jesus and Mary's arms I am free to weep, to mourn, to grieve. Free of hate, free of fear, free of despair, I can weep.

Now is the time that I understand through Boo's experience what Jesus had to endure, and what Mary had to stand helplessly by and accept. Having a God who has faced such death and a Mother who knows the grief of losing a loved one, my faith has matured because I am grounded in it in the most intimate way a person can experience. Our faith does not make sense without suffering and death. Our suffering and death do not make sense without Jesus. And because of that, our solace has no limitations.

That is how I can get up every day with a true sense of joy and peace, even in the midst of this great sorrow. I know my daughter *will* be healed and *will* know deep joy again. I can turn to Jesus and Mary again and again in my sorrow. I can weep and tell Jesus, "This hurts," and I can hear him in my soul. I can hear Mary, too, saying,

"I know."

So this year when we celebrated Easter, and every time I experience the grief of Good Friday with my daughter's illness, I cannot help but anticipate the joy of resurrection. It's not something Pollyanna-ish that I have conjured in my mind. It's grounded in hard-spent grief: and the acceptance of this grief; the acceptance of the grief of the Mother of God and the true acceptance of the suffering of her Son.

Petitions have been prayed. Now I offer up Boo's illness, suffering and death for the salvation of others and for their many little intentions, sorrow and grief. In this way, Boo's little life has meaning and transformative power. She is a living saint. She's never had the opportunity to commit sin. And though I may ask God to let this cup pass from her, I can accept it as God's will and use it for the good of others by offering it up through Jesus, with Jesus and in Jesus.

And that has helped me deal with an unexpected aspect of Boo's illness. It pained me to learn that while I had come to accept her diagnosis and her impending death, I hadn't yet come to terms with accepting her suffering. Oh, sure, I could accept Christ's, but my baby's?

Suffering without redemption is hell. Who can live in hell? I cannot. Boo's suffering is redemptive when I offer it up with Jesus'. Now, every cough and spasm she has is not torture alone, but salvation for others.

It is love, sacrificial love, redeeming love. The world may never know of this little saint, but she will have done great things in her suffering, things worthy of the spirit of Boo, which has always been sheer spunk and hearty laughter and just an absolute zeal for life. I cannot think of a better comfort and support for both the sick and the caregiver than redemptive suffering.

Acceptance is hard; it hurts. But you will find a willing, loving Mother and a compassionate Savior waiting at the foot of this cross. They will help you bear it and see you through to a life of abundant joy and blessings now and in eternity.

I'd like to write that everything is going to be okay. It will be, but there is suffering to embrace that I cannot run from. Without Jesus' life, example and presence, it is impossible to do. But with Him, it can be done, and there can be a sense of peace and joy even in the midst of sorrow.

Allow your child's illness and suffering to transform you. You will be amazed and awed and find incredible strength. Nothing but the real life passion of our loved ones (except our own) can put us so easily within the grasp of Jesus' passion.

Lisa Barker is the author of Just because Your Kids Drive You Insane...Doesn't Mean You Are a Bad Parent! *and* Before I Had Kids I Was a Size 9. *Her books are collections of the parenting humor column,* Jelly Mom, *2004-2009. Lisa lives in California with her husband and four children where she has published her first novel,* Inheritance.

Her beloved Rebecca entered heaven on July 11, 2010. Lisa had offered her suffering for the success of this book.

Eileen and Sadie Haupt

Chapter 2

Sadie's Story

by Eileen Haupt

When I was pregnant with my second baby at the age of 39, I remember considering whether or not to undergo amniocentesis, and having my husband say to me "Trust Jesus." I didn't have a strong faith back then and took this to mean, "Trust Him that nothing would be wrong." But what I came to learn is, that trust really means, "Trust Him, even when the unexpected happens."

I declined prenatal testing as I did during my first pregnancy, not really thinking my baby would have Down syndrome. I am thankful I was never pressured by my doctor to undergo testing. I have spoken to mothers who did discover their baby had Down syndrome through prenatal testing, and most of them have told me, "I wish I didn't know." Although there can be medical reasons why knowing ahead of time might be an advantage, it can also cause a lot of anxiety. And although prenatal testing can tell you a lot about your baby, it cannot tell you the joy your special child will bring.

There are simply no words to express this joy. Sadie's presence has been one of the greatest blessings of my life. She was born two days before Christmas in 1998. Although I didn't hear any cries as they whisked her off to another table (to giver her oxygen, I later discovered), I didn't have any idea anything was awry. I remember so clearly looking at her beautiful face for the first time after the doctor placed her in my arms. I immediately thought to myself, "Oh my gosh, she has Down syndrome!" I just knew. She looked like any other newborn baby, but her eyes were just a bit puffy. I said, "Her eyes look funny," to my husband Steve, but he attributed it to the birth process. I thought to myself, "No, that's not it." It was a very surreal moment. For an instant, I felt like my whole life up to then had prepared me for that moment.

Some minutes later, the doctor told me the pediatrician would be in to check up on Sadie, but the residents "suspect she has Down syndrome." I just said," I know." Somehow, I was not shocked. I am so grateful Sadie "told" me first, through her eyes, which cushioned the news for me. It was as though she and I had an intimate and silent conversation with our eyes. Had it not been for that experience, I think I would have been more shocked at hearing the words. Even in my fallen-away state, God still gave me the grace to bear the news.

I did not seem to go through a grieving process like many other mothers do, but snapped into reality while still in the hospital. Not that I wasn't emotional about it, but my bouts of "why me?" were short-lived. Although my faith was not strong at that time, there were a few things which helped me adjust. The most important was Sadie "telling me."

Another was that I knew of families who had healthy children, but by accident or disease became parents of children with special needs overnight. I realized there are no guarantees when it comes to our children. Anything can happen, at any time. Ours just happened early on.

Learning that there is a waiting list for babies with Down syndrome was also helpful in accepting her diagnosis. The only difference between those adoptive parents and us is that we didn't ask for it. But I knew if anyone could do this, Steve and I could. Steve's daughters, Bridget and Hannah, didn't bat an eyelash when they came to visit us in the hospital and we told them the news. "That's okay, we'll love her," is all they said. And they have. And our daughter Colleen, who is almost 2 years older than Sadie has always been an amazing big sister.

It is routine in our hospital to have a pediatric cardiologist examine newborns diagnosed with Down syndrome, because of the high incidence of heart defects. The echocardiogram showed that Sadie had a complete atrioventricular (AV) canal defect, which required surgery within six months. So at the tender age of 3 months, Sadie underwent open-heart surgery at Children's Hospital in Boston. Thankfully, the surgery went well, and she has been healthy ever since.

When Sadie was an infant, I learned that 90 percent of babies prenatally diagnosed with Down syndrome are aborted. I nearly fell off my chair when I read this statistic. I had been "personally pro-life" through most of my adult life, but thought, "Who am I to tell other women what to do?" But this was the moment at which I awakened to the tragedy of abortion. By asking questions and educating myself in the facts about abortion, I finally became unabashedly pro-life and knew I needed to actively work toward making abortion illegal.

I began to notice the messages in magazines and on television with an underlying expectation of undergoing amnio and aborting if the baby was found to have a genetic condition. I remember watching a segment on the *Today Show* in which a gynecologist was discussing the topic of, "Who should have an amnio." The doctor said something to the effect of, "And then if there is a problem, you can decide whether or not to keep the pregnancy," as if these babies were simply disposable objects. I cried through the segment as I looked at my beautiful infant daughter, and thought, "Why? Why wouldn't anyone want her?" I wrote a letter to the gynecologist with some suggestions on how she could revise her talk the next time, and copied Katie Couric. (I heard back from neither.) That letter gave birth to an activist!

Since the day of Sadie's birth, I have seen myself as an advocate for her and for others who have Down syndrome. I want people to see that I am okay with who she is, so they will see that it is not a negative thing, and that she is very much loved. My way of dealing with her diagnosis was to talk about it. Whenever I'd be out in public and someone would admire her, as people do with newborns, I would feel compelled to say,

"She has Down syndrome." Sometimes I would get, "yes, I know." And sometimes I got, "I have a nephew with Down syndrome," or some other family member. It was amazing to me the number of people I met who had a connection to someone who had Down syndrome.

Sadie's birth sowed a seed that eventually brought me fully back to my Catholic faith. Up until then, I saw my husband as the faithful one. I had fallen away from the Faith for 20 years, and although I had begun attending Mass occasionally about a year earlier, I was still far away. Looking back, I can see a trail of events that Sadie's birth put into action to guide me back. I can see God's hand in all of it. Not only did I return, but also my Protestant husband came into the Catholic Church during the Easter Vigil two years ago. So the blessings keep coming!

I have prayed that God would use me to educate about, and advocate for, individuals with Down syndrome. He has answered my prayer, and then some! The fire of faith caught on and God put many opportunities in my path, mostly through the pro-life community. It has been an amazing ride! I have been able to speak to groups, participate in programs to educate medical students, write articles, speak at the National Right to Life Convention, appear on TV and radio talk shows, and talk to parents who have just learned of their baby's diagnosis.

The most fun and rewarding experience has been to co-found Keep Infants with Down Syndrome (KIDS) with Leticia Velasquez. This was an inspiration on both of our parts to form a group of parents and their children with Down syndrome to walk together in the annual March for Life in Washington, D.C. The purpose for forming this group was to raise awareness of the tragically high incidence of abortion among babies with Down syndrome, and to challenge the negativity toward them by showing how our children are loved by their families.

Through Leticia's internet contacts, we have been able to reach many families. We had about 40 people join us for our first event at the 2009 March for Life. We were able to visit with Congresswoman Cathy McMorris Rodgers in her office after the March. In 2010, we were honored to have Cathy attend our event with her son Cole, an adorable preschooler with Down syndrome. The National Right to Life Committee generously allows our group to meet at their headquarters and provides us with lunch and refreshments before the March.

It recently occurred to me that out of the several hundred thousand pro-lifers participating in the D.C. march, and out of the thousands of schools, churches, organizations, and associations that are represented, KIDS was probably the only organization representing a group of babies that were actually sought out to be aborted for who they are.

If only a mother expecting a special needs child could know whom her child really is. If only she could feel the joy and the love that she will feel for her baby if she welcomes her into the world. If only she knew how many hearts would be changed by her special baby's presence. If only she knew, she would never abort.

My plea to parents who have just learned that their unborn baby has Down syndrome is this: It is natural to feel fear and sadness when you get the diagnosis. And if you abort your baby, you may get rid of the fear; but the sadness will always be there. Always. If you welcome your baby into the world, you will find that the reality is nothing like you feared, and your special baby will transform your sadness into joy.

Be not afraid!

Eileen and her family live in Vermont, where she has been a candidate for State Representative. She is a delegate for the National Right to Life Committee and presented on Down syndrome for NRTL National Convention. She is a freelance writer and co-founder of KIDS. She and Leticia appeared as guests on the EWTN program. "Faith and Culture" hosted by Colleen Carroll-Campbell.

Barbara and Jon Curtis

Chapter 3

A Little Extra

by Barbara Curtis

My son Jonathan has a little extra. A little extra enthusiasm, a little extra innocence, a little extra charm. Oh, and did I mention an extra chromosome? The one on the 21st pair that inspires so much fear in parents-to-be.

I suppose at one time I was fearful about Down syndrome. But in 1993, when they placed the blue-blanketed bundle in my arms and I could see he looked, well, just a little different, I actually felt a sense of awe. Here will be a challenge, so many things to learn.

It helped that we already had a few "normal" children. But other things had opened my heart as well. There was Amy, a 6-year-old cutie pie we babysat for now and then. Amy's dad had left shortly after her birth—just couldn't get into having a daughter with Down syndrome.

On the brighter side was the dad and daughter duo I'd seen a month before, riding the merry-go-round. A gleeful, almond-eyed 3-year-old, a father helplessly in love.

There's something special here, I thought. In this society, for a parent without one to see something positive in a child with Down syndrome requires a paradigm shift, I know. But if my counterculture years taught me anything, it was to question prevailing attitudes. I'd really never liked the dread surrounding Down syndrome, clouding the horizon for still-waiting-for-test-results expectant parents.

On the internet in recent years, I've "met" a few who've received the dreaded news, then logged onto Down syndrome newsgroups, trying to pick up the pieces. Often they describe pressure from geneticists and doctors to terminate the pregnancy and "try again." These professionals are quick to point out the burdens of having a child with trisomy 21: possible medical problems, heavier emotional demands, and a child who is "less than." But then on the Internet, or face-to-face in their own home towns, they meet the real professionals - parents involved with Down syndrome on a daily basis. They are in a much better position to comment on the so-called "quality of life" issues. Always there is an outpouring of loving response, personal variations on Emily Kingsley's theme in her famous essay, "Welcome to Holland": So you planned to go to Italy and landed in unexpected territory. At first you're disappointed. Then you notice the windmills and the tulips - beauty you never expected to find. You discover it's not a bad place after all.

My own son Jonny, now 7, is a snappy dresser, an avid film buff, and a splendid host. He loves playing soccer and hearing both sides cheer whenever he kicks a goal. At home or school he is the first to offer help, to comfort someone who's down, and to laugh uproariously at the punch lines.

His preschool teacher named him Ambassador of Goodwill. His public school Kindergarten teacher, after 30 plus years of teaching, said she'd never seen children as loving and caring as Jonny's classmates. The secret, she said, was Jonny. When he graduated from her class, she wrote us: "As the Bible says, 'The Lord does not look at the things man looks at. Man looks at the outward appearance, but the Lord looks at the heart' (1 Samuel 16:7 NIV). Jonny certainly taught the children and me to look at the heart; for he has a very big heart!"

Both confirmed what I'd seen all along. Jonny has a way of breaking the ice before others can think too long about their response to a child who is, well, just a little different. Then he brings out the best in them. In fact, I bet some people would rather spend a day with Jonathan than with the experts who question his right to exist. There's Princeton professor/bioethicist Peter Singer, urging the right (or duty) of parents to terminate the life of a disabled child up to 28 days after birth. Or Bob Edwards, world-renowned embryologist, predicting it will soon be a "sin" (his term) for parents to give birth to children with disabilities.

This would seem a giant step back for our enlightened society, which a generation ago ceased banishing children with Down syndrome to institutions, making it possible for them to grow into productive members of society. In a culture working overtime to root out prejudice and prosecute hate, these "expert" voices sound suspiciously supremacist. But maybe it's just that they suffer from their own undiagnosed disabilities blinded by a caste system of individuals based on I.Q., educability, and earning potential. Paralyzed within their "perfect" paradigms.

Having a child with Down syndrome has helped me see there's infinitely more to life than intelligence, beauty and "perfection." It's also taught me that not everything can be measured in dollars and cents the benefits of full-inclusion extend beyond a child with Down syndrome to his classmates, teachers, family and friends.

Before Jonny's birth, I'd prepared announcements with a line from Elizabeth Barrett Browning: "God's gifts put man's best dreams to shame." I sent them proudly, adding a note about his extra chromosome and our great love for him. (One friend's comment: "Well, Barbara, he'll never be president, but isn't that just as well?" And this was 1992!)

He's been a gift I never would have thought to ask for, bringing lessons I never knew I needed to learn. The greatest surprise is this: Our life together has been less about my helping him reach his potential than about him helping me reach mine.

Sometimes when we're in a museum or a mall, in the middle of a good laugh, I catch someone off-guard, looking uncomfortable and standoffish. I know that as long as we live some will see Jonny as having a little less. I've learned he has a little more. And so does our world because he's here.

Twelve years later, Jonny has continued to spread joy everywhere he goes. So many things he's good at: basketball, baseball, swimming, horseback riding. The guy everyone wants to dance with, Jonny was voted Homecoming King by his peers in his senior year. Following graduation, Jonny is working part time at a Habitat for Humanity ReStore while continuing to develop his job skills.

Barbara Curtis is a writer who has produced over 600 articles for Focus on the Family, Christian Parenting Today, Chicken Soup for the Christian Woman's Soul, World, and many other publications. She writes a biweekly newspaper column and has received three prestigious Am Awards. Previous books include Small Beginnings, and Ready Set Read! Barbara and her husband Tripp are the parents of twelve children, nine who still reside with them in Waterford, Virginia. Web site: www.barbaracurtis.com.

Mary and Peter Kellett

Chapter 4

Peter's Story

by Mary Kellett

When I found out I was pregnant with my son Peter, I remember feeling a wave of love and peace wash over me. None of the familiar fears and questions entered my mind. Questions like; How am I going to handle another baby? or How is my health going to be? We were already blessed with 10 children and I was 43 years old. I remember thinking that God was truly with me and that this baby was special. Little did I know the plans the Lord had in mind for the sweet child we named Peter.

A routine ultrasound at 19 weeks identified markers for a chromosomal condition called trisomy 18. I started to cry as the doctor described trisomy 18 and said there were no survivors beyond two weeks. An amniocentesis was recommended to confirm the diagnosis and to help us with our "choices."

We declined, not wanting to risk hurting our baby. The only choice for us was to love him and care for him as long as God allowed us the blessing of his life. We found out he was a boy and knew he would need a strong name, so we named him Peter, which means "Rock."

The pregnancy continued with frequent monitoring and pressure to have an amnio. I remember saying again and again that I did not need to know. I was at peace with God's plan. I felt I was carried through those months on sheer grace from the Lord. At 33 weeks Peter's movement was slowing down and an emergency C-section was performed. Peter was immediately baptized after birth and confirmed two days later. Test results showed he did indeed have trisomy 18. Doctors recommended that we stop treatment, wrap him up in a blanket and let him die. When our daughter brought us photos she found online of older children and adults living with trisomy 18, we asked the doctor why he had said there were no survivors beyond two weeks. The doctor calmly told us that they had to think about resources, and that Peter would never contribute to society. His life would be filled with pain and suffering and he would be a terrible burden to our family and our other children.

One of the most painful conversations we had was with a female doctor whom we had never met before Peter's birth. She told me that she wanted to talk to me as a mother, and that if I wanted to be a good mother to Peter I would let him go. I just cried silently. After talking with our pastor and the hospital chaplain, both very holy priests, and after learning that Peter's heart was stable and functional, we went against the doctor's recommendation and decided to keep treating Peter. He was showing us his strong will to live, and we loved him and insisted on the same care a "normal" child would receive.

Peter came home to our large, active, loving family, and instead of being a burden, he became a source of tremendous grace and the best blessing, next to our Catholic faith. He is a happy, sweet little boy who gives us unlimited love and is greatly loved and treasured in return. Peter has become our teacher in so many ways. I call him and other children with special needs, "Teachers of our Souls." He has taught us to love life in a deeper way and to trust in God's wisdom and providence. He has taught us that there are many ways to contribute to society, and that he contributes in the most important way possible: by helping us become better, more compassionate, caring people. Along with the Holy Spirit, Peter inspired the founding of Prenatal Partners for Life. a non-profit, pro-life support group to help other families who receive an adverse diagnosis. The Lord has turned our tears and pain into love and support for others.

Peter is now 6 years old and continues to be a great joy and blessing. Throughout his life, God has held us very close to Him, giving us the strength and grace to seek His will in caring for Peter. There have been challenges, with Peter receiving the same care as anyone else would. When Peter was younger he caught RSV one winter and had to be hospitalized. When we were asked what we wanted done if he ran into trouble breathing, we asked what the normal care would be for any of our other children. We were told that they would be put on a ventilator to give their lungs a rest. We said that we wanted the same care to be given to Peter. Two doctors stated that they could not believe we wanted to put Peter through that, making it seem like we were cruel for what they termed aggressive treatment for Peter, but would be called normal care for others. Peter did have to be put on a vent for a few days, but got better and came home. And since then, he has been a ring bearer in three of his sisters' weddings. Thankfully as Peter has gotten older these trials have become less frequent, with more doctors understanding the great blessing and gift Peter is to us.

We try and keep Peter out of the hospital when he is sick, treating him as much as possible at home. A short time before Peter's second birthday, he caught a cold which turned into pneumonia. We wanted to keep him at home, so we started treatment, both medical and spiritual. We have always had wonderful support from our parish and many priests and religious friends and family. We asked for prayers that Peter would get better, and I started a novena to St. Therese, the "Little Flower."

A few days before Peter's birthday, I finished the novena. Sometimes St. Therese will give you a rose to let you know she has heard your prayer. I wondered if I would get a rose. Peter's birthday came and we had a party for him. Our daughter Teresa was engaged to be married, and Brandon, her fiancé, was bringing his parents to Peter's party to meet us for the first time. Brandon's mom walked up to me and Peter and handed us a beautiful red rose. She told us she was in a florist shop that day and there was a sign that said, "If your name is Peter ask for a rose." It was the most beautiful, perfect rose, with gold sparkles deep down in the petals. St. Therese had heard our prayers and gave Peter a rose for his birthday. Peter did get better, and the Little Flower continues to be a great friend and intercessor for him, along with Mary, our Blessed Mother, and all the saints of Heaven.

When I reflect on what Peter has done for me personally, I am profoundly grateful. He has deepened my faith and has made me see things in a different light. He has kept me very close to God, teaching me a more eternal perspective on life. Peter has helped me to be more detached from the world. I think it is because he lives so close to Heaven and is so close to the Lord. He has caused me to turn my gaze toward Heaven and to always have hope. I have also met some of the nicest people because of Peter, many of whom have become dear friends. I have learned to trust in God's will and to seek it and accept it, even though it may not be mine. When Peter gets sick, I have learned to place him in our Blessed Mother's arms, asking her to take care of Peter for me and, if it is God's will, for her to give him back to me. I have learned that, as hard as the cross can be, God's grace IS sufficient. I have learned that, as much as I and my family love Peter, God loves him even more.

We don't know how long God will allow Peter to be with us here on earth, but we don't know the length of any of our lives, do we? We do know that God is always faithful. And we know that each and every life has a purpose and a plan. We are all created by God in His image and likeness. We all have a place in the great tapestry of life. When we cut life short by abortion, infanticide or euthanasia we put holes in God's tapestry and we weaken the fabric of life and of all society. When we embrace and cherish all life, we allow God's beautiful design for His tapestry to be realized and for society and the world to be strengthened and transformed by His love. We all have a part to play. There is a special place in the world for all of God's creation, including those who are differently-abled. Peter has taught us that they have the most important place of all because the lessons they teach us are spiritual and will bear eternal fruit. The world desperately needs the blessings and lessons that these precious children bring.

We are truly blessed to have a living saint, pure and sinless, as part of our family. When well-meaning people sometimes dwell on all the things little Peter may never do, I always think of how he will never, ever sin. He will never make the Lord sad or the angels weep. He will never make me worry about his eternal salvation. I pray that I and all of my children and loved ones will be with God for all eternity in Heaven. I don't have to pray that prayer for Peter. He is leading the way to Heaven for all of us.

Mary Kellett lives in Minnesota with her husband, Don, their 11 children and eight grandchildren. Mary is the Director of Prenatal Partners for Life, a life-affirming support group for families that receive an adverse diagnosis for their child before or after birth. Please visit www.prenatalpartnersforlife.org or call 763-772-3868 for more information.

Tamara and Mary Faith Musella

Chapter 5

Love Conquers All

by Tamara Musella

Hello, my name is Mom, formerly known as Tamara. I was conceived, out of wedlock, unaccepted, and hidden from society. I was adopted by two loving parents, who after just finishing a 50-day Novena to our Mother Mary asking to be blessed with a child, received a phone call that I was born and needed a family. I was baptized a Roman Catholic and made my First Holy Communion and sometime after that my family stopped going to church.

I was raised without truly knowing God. The only thing close to knowing God was my mother's Italian parents, who lived in Brooklyn, NY. Their living room was a glass-enclosed shrine to the Blessed Mother, Jesus and all the saints. Statues, various colored rosary beads for every occasion, and the Bible. As a child, all I could do was sit on the plastic-covered couch and look around, knowing that I had to be on best behavior in this room.

My Grandpa Costantino and tragic life experiences in my teenage years are what brought me back, crying on my knees, to the Church. I was about 20 years old. It was truly God calling me and leading a lost and scared sheep home. From that moment on, I knew this was where I was meant to be.

In 1999, I was a happily married woman involved in my local parish. I gave birth to a beautiful baby boy. We had all the blessings a new family could have. A healthy young couple, we owned our own house with a white picket fence and dog. It was a Kodak moment. But it was not to last; in the following years, we suffered three miscarriages, all baby girls who died of severe chromosomal abnormalities within the first trimester. Life was no longer going the way we planned. In 2002, I received a call from my general practitioner with my annual check-up results. He was thrilled and said "You're pregnant!" I began to cry and handed the phone to my husband, who had to explain my reaction.

Faced with uncertainty and despair, I walked into my obstetrician's office. They monitored me almost daily for the next couple of months. When the doctors told me they suspected the baby had Down syndrome, something I had only vaguely heard of, I just began to cry. Chromosomal damage was the words I had heard before—words which had come to mean pain. As wounded and confused as I was, I knew I was going to do everything I could to help this baby survive. I also thought I would have everyone's support. This would prove to be a fantasy.

My husband and I agreed to prenatal testing. Our daughter's heart was not growing and forming properly, but all else seemed to be okay. The next four-and-a-half months were terrifying, lonely, and confusing. I had been labeled "The woman carrying a Down syndrome baby" and my baby had been labeled "Down syndrome." I felt isolated and distant from family, friends and doctors. People looked at me with pity. I felt as if I were dropped off on a deserted island with sharks circling waiting to take this baby from me. The doctors wanted to take her from inside of me and then discard her in the garbage behind the doctor's office. My baby in the garbage! I had to find the strength to see this through. I talked, cried,

23

and sang to my precious baby girl all night and day. I rubbed my belly to make contact with the life that was moving inside of me. I wanted to assure her that Mommy loved her and no matter what, she was the love of my life.

Our emotions and thoughts play tricks on us all. You're as strong as an eagle and then as weak as cornered prey. You're confident and then terrified. Your faith in God is everlasting and then destroyed by Satan's whisperings.

My husband and I drifted slowly and quietly away from each other – physically and emotionally. He was in such turmoil at times that his remarks about the pregnancy and the baby were too painful for me to endure, and we couldn't be in the same room. I was desperate and would contemplate abortion at times. I looked back at "the Kodak moments" when it was just me, my husband and our son, and wondered how this had happened to our perfect family.

Tears would slowly roll down my cheeks as I crept into our son's room and gently kissed him while he slept peacefully, then I would slide into bed, trying not to wake my husband; yet another night when we did not even say "good night" or "I love you" to each other.

Our son was about 4 years old at this time and excited about having a baby in the house. I gently explained that, when the baby was born, our days would be filled with many doctor appointments and hospital stays. He took whatever information his little brain needed and left the rest behind. A lesson all adults should learn!

Family and friends continued to assault me with the dreadful stories of psychiatric wards filled with adults with Down syndrome. Their words of emptiness and misfortune spoke of how this baby would not become anything but completely dependent on me for the rest of her life. The doctors and nurses looked on me with only pity and never once took the time to give me any support or even a smile. They swayed me to go to speak to their genetic counselor, who proved to only have one motive - to abort the baby. I never saw that cold, unfeeling genetic counselor again.

We began to pray constantly for our baby and family. My mom was optimistic and would try to cheer me up by saying, "Just think pink!" Unfortunately she was very ill and had to live out of state near a hospital that could take care of her. Yet despite that, she always did her best to be support me. For my dad I think it was more difficult, although he always supported me as well. His little brother had been born with Down syndrome. When he was four years old, he was taken from his home and placed in an institution, and my dad never saw his little brother again. His brother became very ill and died around six years old, in the institution, away from his family. It seemed as though my father was scared for me and this baby, dreading that I would be put through similar suffering and pain, but he never wanted to talk about it.

I would say the Rosary daily at a peaceful time. My husband would come and sit in the room and take in the serenity that only God could give him. I could feel the Holy Spirit lifting and enveloping me like a baby in His arms. St. Gerard, the patron saint of expectant mothers, became my personal friend and spiritual companion. Our Blessed Mother Mary became my mother, and St. Anne became my grandmother, gazing at me with loving eyes of aged wisdom and understanding.

The day finally came when the contractions began; Mary Faith had decided that at 3 a.m. she wanted to enter the world! Although my husband was there, I decided to pack my bag, kiss him and tell him to stay home with our son. "I'm going to the hospital by myself," I said, and drove myself to the emergency room. Needless to say, the security guard was startled by the sight of a pregnant woman driving fiercely into the parking lot!

After a quick examination, it seemed as though the baby wanted out, but was stuck in the wrong position! "Ugh!" I smiled to myself and whispered to her "Cut it out, Mary Faith! Let's not start our life off together like this!" They told me to call my husband before they began the C-section. He had 15 minutes before they started to prep me.

The procedure was starting and I was alone and scared, yet excited to finally hold my baby. The moment had come. I was surrounded by strange doctors and nurses, under glaring lights and stand-by emergency equipment. No medications were given to me except to numb the area of the surgery. Yet somehow, I began to feel oddly peaceful and calm. It was pure spiritual calm. God, his angels and saints were there. I felt them holding me and kissing my forehead. The warmth and love was more than any earthly words could describe. My child was going to be born in the sight of God.

At that moment, my husband walked in, and all I could see above his surgical mask were his eyes, the eyes of a man still searching for peace. He held my hand and listened to each order the doctor was giving to his staff. A moment later, a sweet cry echoed throughout the sterile room. Our Mary Faith's beautiful voice was like that of an angel! They whisked her away before we got a good look at her. All I saw was a very tiny, round head, a cute button nose, beautiful eyes, and tiny lips all tightly swaddled in a blanket. She had arrived! My husband kissed me. Our lives were forever changed at that moment. Our love for Mary Faith was exploding.

The next five days I was a mother lioness protecting her cub. Mary Faith had tubes coming out of her little body from head to toe, machines watching her every move. As my husband slowly and cautiously walked into the NICU, he looked at his child with tremendous love as a tear fell from his eye. He sat down, held his daughter, looked in her eyes, and with gentleness and love, fed her a bottle. He kissed her little forehead and became "Daddy". He was reborn that very moment to become the daddy that would never let anyone or anything ever hurt his daughter. That has never changed. She is, to this day, his beautiful, funny princess.

Mary Faith will light up a room with her presence, despite the tilted halo of mischief that she has acquired through the years. My mom was able to spend the first year of Mary Faith's life holding and loving her. Shortly after her first birthday my mom was called to Heaven. Everybody loves Mary Faith, and not because they feel they have to, but because they truly do. She is accepted for exactly who she is--God's gift.

Having a child with Down syndrome is just like having any other child. You have good days and not so good days. Days where learning is easy for them and days when learning something is going to be harder. There a smiles and tantrums. Some days they are obedient and other days they are disobedient. They love their siblings and they fight with their siblings. Mary is not our daughter with Down syndrome

. . . Mary is just Mary; our blonde haired, whimsical, funny, smart, loving daughter and Michael's silly little sister, all wrapped up as our gift from God.

Tamara lives on Long Island with her family where they are actively involved in a Catholic Homeschooling group, volunteering at their parish, and with the local Down syndrome sports and family activities. She can be reached at tmmc4me@aol.com anytime for help, guidance, and a shoulder to lean on.

Peter and Janet Olesen

Chapter 6

St. Joseph and the Second Gift

by Janet M. Olesen

My husband and I waited a year after our marriage before we tried to have children. I had been terribly sick with chronic depression, an illness I was desperately afraid to pass on to a child. He finally convinced me that we, better than most, would be able to care for a child with mental illness, to understand him and to help him grow into adulthood. But I never stopped asking God, throughout my pregnancy, to spare my child from chronic depression. I begged that our baby might be born healthy and happy, although I always added "Thy will be done." It wasn't a prayer to ensure God's presence in any outcome; I added that request because I felt ill equipped and unworthy to determine and take responsibility for the make-up of another human being—as though God would let me do that!

God's will was that our beautiful son, Peter, would be born with Asperger's syndrome, a mild form of autism, and that I would have the ability to recognize that there was a problem well before my son's symptoms became obvious to others. God also gave me the strength to pursue help for him despite the difficulties. Peter cried desperately and often for the first three months of his life. Then his pediatrician diagnosed acid reflux disease, and medication and a weighted formula alleviated his pain.

One bright morning, when Peter was still less than a month old, I rocked him through an hour of agonized crying. I prayed to God for help, tears streaming down my own face. I felt, in answer, the need to choose a saint to help me care for Peter. Immediately, St. Joseph came to mind. I had always admired this quiet saint who protected Baby Jesus as if He were his own. I knew that St. Joseph would guard and carefully guide my Peter in the same way. As the months and then years passed, I would give Peter over to St. Joseph whenever I became overwhelmed and unable to meet his needs. I always felt comforted.

Peter's crying began again at nine months. This time, however, it was brought on by frustration or disappointment. One afternoon, when he was about a year old, I watched Peter try to push a car sideways. When it would not roll, he began to scream and cry; he did not stop for almost two hours.

Peter didn't seem interested in other children, although he was fascinated by their toys. Once, when he was 2-and-a-half, Peter saw two boys playing with trucks in a sandbox at the park. He grinned and toddled straight for the dump truck. The boys frowned and told him, "No! We don't want you!" but Peter repeatedly reached for the truck, the smile never leaving his face. It was as though he didn't see or hear them.

For eight years, we stumbled through a maze of doctors, therapists and social skills groups, trying to find a reason for the lengthy crying episodes, his clumsiness, oversensitivity, allergies, peculiar vocabulary and lack of social intelligence. He was released, too soon, I thought, from our school district's early intervention program to go to Kindergarten. At the same time, though, he found a second home in a local martial arts studio. On the wall behind the teacher's desk, I noticed there hung a small picture of the Sacred Heart. The familiar image of Our Lord gave me a sense of comfort.

At the studio, Peter progressed more slowly than the other students, but he had a passion and dedication that parents of children with Asperger's will find familiar. His teacher, Soke, took Peter's incessant, multi-syllabic, wordy chatter in stride, but taught him to listen well. He never remarked on Peter's awkwardness; instead, he spoke proudly of each small improvement in balance and coordination that Peter made. Peter's attachment to ju-jitsu and the constant support of his teacher created an area of his life where he could have consistent, albeit small, successes—and the knowledge that he was of value.

In school, he faced a daily battle of learning to write legibly, along with the constant bullying of his schoolmates. Once, when the teasing on the bus became too much for him, Peter put a choke-hold on his tormentor. He ran home from the bus stop and up to his room, where I found him sobbing, face down on the bed. He was afraid of what he had done. I called Soke, and brought Peter to speak with him the next day. I never found out what was said, but Peter left the studio calmer, ready to accept the consequences of his actions and more devoted to his teacher than ever. Peter considered Soke his hero, and often repeated his teacher's advice and directives at home. Soke's given name, I learned with a tingling of recognition, is Joseph.

At the age of 10, Peter was awarded his black belt in ju-jitsu. His father, sister and I watched with great pride as Peter tied the cloth around himself for the first time, a grin pushing at his cheeks despite his efforts to maintain a solemn expression. Peter couldn't wait for the next school day because he finally has a small group of friends who say "That's great!" when something good happens to him. He has come a long way, thanks in no small part to the guardianship of two Josephs. I have come a long way, too. I am no longer afraid to bring my needs before God because I know that every gift He grants comes with a second gift—the means to embrace the first.

Janet is a stay-at-home mom and part time music teacher. She has two children, Peter, 13 and Hannah, 11. She and her husband, Bob, live in Huntington on Long Island, NY. Their favorite past-time is sailing with the children.

Tom and Christopher Royals

Chapter 7

A Faith Deepens Down Under

by Therese Royals

Our story begins in September 2000, when my husband, Steve, was offered a teaching job at a school in the South East of South Australia. As we prepared to move to a new town in January 2001, I discovered that we were expecting baby number six. I was excited by the news, but felt a bit overwhelmed by all that was changing in our lives. Little did I know that more significant changes lay ahead.

In December, we packed up our five children and moved to Millicent. In January, Steve started working at the school, and we enrolled our older three children--Daniel, 9; Sam, 7; and Madeline 6--there as students. Our youngest, Brigette, 3, and Tom, 1, stayed home with me.

I loved living in the country with a town nearby. I loved my days at home with Brigette and Tom. We established a new routine quickly. Everything seemed to be going well until the end of March, when Tom got very sick. At first, I thought he had a stomach virus. He was vomiting and breathing so quickly that he couldn't shut his mouth. He was extremely thirsty and seemed hungry all the time. After several days like this, his arms and legs turned blue. I was concerned, but didn't realize how seriously ill Tom was.

Two days before his diagnosis, I was speaking with my mother on the phone, and she convinced me that I needed to speak with a doctor that night. I phoned the doctor on call and told her what was happening. She advised me to give Tom plenty of fluids and to bring him in the following morning. The next day, I took him to the doctor. She was very concerned about the color of his limbs and an awful diaper rash he had from the high sugars in his body and frequent urination. She weighed him, gave me a prescription for diaper rash cream and told me to keep giving him extra fluids. I was to bring him back the next day. In the 24 hours that followed, we gave Tom plenty to drink. When we went back the next morning, he had lost over one kilogram, or about two pounds, in weight. At that point, I knew something was seriously wrong.

That afternoon, doctors diagnosed Tom with type one diabetes, and we were flown south to the city of Adelaide by the Royal Flying Doctors. During our first few days in Adelaide, doctors kept Tom in intensive care. Then he was transferred to a regular room until he was well enough to come home. During the week we were there, I received training on how to care for Tom.

Having a child with diabetes has had an impact on every aspect of our lives. Our days are full of blood sugar tests, and treating sugar highs and sugar lows. We need to weigh any piece of food that contains carbohydrates. Then we calculate how much insulin Tom needs to process that amount. Into that equation we factor any exercise he does, since that will also affect his blood sugar levels. Sometimes his levels rise, but we are unable to determine why. Other times, we cannot bring it down, no matter how hard we try. That is when we get nervous. We test for blood ketones because high levels can cause dehydration. If that happens, we need to rehydrate him with an intravenous drip.

When we travel, we take a bag with pump supplies, injections, glucose tablets and extra insulin. If we forget to take that bag, Tom's life can be in danger. Not a day goes by that we don't think about diabetes and Tom's needs. Whenever we have a hard day, I find myself asking God why we have to deal with this. I complain about the unfairness of life. But I know deep in my heart that God has used Tom and diabetes to teach me many life lessons and to deepen my faith.

I have learned that we do not suffer in vain. So, I no longer fear suffering the way I once did. I have seen God's love and mercy, and understand more fully why He allows crosses and trials. I have come to see the importance of community; we need to rely on each other in times of need. I have seen that God provides for all our needs. Through everything, I have learned perseverance and the value of every human life. The world tells us that suffering is to be avoided at all costs. While I admit that I still don't like suffering, my attitude towards it has changed. I can see how necessary it is in our journey toward wholeness.

When Tom was in intensive care and needed an intravenous drip, I could see that he was healed through the pain. He was made whole. At the time, I remember holding his arm still and seeing the look of terror on his face. I felt as though I was betraying him as he screamed. He didn't know that he would die a painful and horrible death if we didn't get the needle into his arm. I realized later that I had felt abandoned and betrayed by God. But I also recognized that maybe God knew what we needed better than I did. I realized that I needed to trust and believe that He was there, helping me through the rough spots and letting things happen to deepen my faith.

While we were in the hospital, I often felt as if God was distant. Looking back later, I saw that He carried me through and looked after every detail. It wasn't until many months later that I realized how much my faith had deepened and that I had a new outlook on life. It was only in writing about these events that I recognized the love and mercy of God.

The day before Tom was flown to Adelaide, my brother had driven up from there to spend the weekend with us. He was able to look after our other four children while Steve and I were at the hospital with Tom. He was also able to take Brigette back to Adelaide for my mother to watch, since Steve needed to return to work. Steve had many people offer him help. One family took Madeline into their home for the week, and many people looked after the boys between the end of classes and the beginning of Steve's vacation. Others made meals for us even after I came back from

Adelaide. Our new daughter, Amelia, born at 39 weeks, proved to be a settled, placid baby. She was very content and rarely cried. And when she did, my other children were happy to help care for her.

These little things showed me that God was helping us through everything. Without Him looking after these little things, our load would have been much harder to carry. God really knows how much we can bear and wants to help us through all our trials. I remember reading the autobiography of St. Therese the Little Flower about six months after Tom's diagnosis. At the end of the book, St. Therese said to one of the sisters, "How very good God is to us. He gives us the strength to endure." Because of my experience with Tom, I know that St. Therese's words are true.

When Tom was first diagnosed, doctors told me that a cure would be discovered during his lifetime. Every day, scientists are making strides toward that goal, using both adult stem cells and embryonic stem cells. Adult stem cells have shown much more promise, but still money is being put into embryonic stem cell research. As a Catholic, I cannot agree with that. Every time an embryo is used to seek a cure, the nucleus is removed, and the child dies.

I would love for Tom to live life without his pump and injections. But I don't want a cure to be found at the cost of another human life. An embryo is another person. Since adult stem cells are showing so much promise, it is my hope that diabetes organizations will put more money into this research. Sadly, some of the major diabetes groups are investing into embryonic stem cell research. Because of this, I am unable to support their fundraising efforts. I simply cannot justify giving money to a group that uses that money to kill embryos, even if it were to bring about a cure for Tom.

Another person should not die so that Tom can live without diabetes. To say that one life has more value than another takes away the dignity of all human life, which should be valued at every stage and in every state. All humans have some disability; some are more obvious than others. Having a child with diabetes has shown me that no matter what others think or say, Tom's life has great value. Today, he is a happy ten-year-old who is doing very well on an insulin pump. Even if a cure is never found, I will still thank God for Tom.

Tom has had diabetes for nine years now. Technology has made it much easier for us to look after him. He uses an insulin pump to keep his blood sugars in range and we have been very happy with this treatment. But we were soon to face another challenge.

Last year in April, our seventh child, Christopher was diagnosed with type one diabetes. He started insulin injections in May and has been very stable since. Although it was a shock, we found out very early and his blood sugars have been very easy to mange. Christopher is still in what is called a honeymoon phase of diabetes. This means that he is still producing insulin himself. Eventually his body will stop producing his own insulin and he will need insulin injections everyday.

The second time around I found much easier since I knew so much about diabetes. There is still that nagging fear that comes from having two children with it. I wondered a couple of times "is this because of something I did or something I failed to do?"

I know that type one diabetes is an autoimmune disease. There is nothing I can do to change this. I also know that God has a plan for Tom, Christopher and our whole family. Part of that plan is carrying the cross that comes with diabetes. Even though it can be a heavy cross at times, God is there helping us carry it. My hope for the future for both Tom and Christopher is that they embrace their cross and that it helps them come to know God in a deeper way.

Therese and her family live in Australia. She blogs s at the Aussie Coffee Shop.

Melissa and 'Wonderboy' Wiley

Chapter 8

The Quiet Joy

by Melissa Wiley

Every noon and every night I lie down with Wonderboy to cuddle him while he falls asleep. I read him a story, turn out the light, and pretend to go to sleep myself. (Okay, *most* of the time I'm pretending...) My two-year-old son, naturally, is not immediately inclined to start snoring. He'd much rather play.

Because he cannot get up by himself, there's no problem keeping him in bed. He simply wants to talk. He babbles away in both verbal speech and sign language, sometimes singing (with vigorous hand motions accompanied by rhythmic grunts), sometimes reliving the book we just read by running through all his favorite animal sounds, and finally, in a last-ditch effort to entice mommy into conversation, by applying heart-melting tactics: "Love Mommy! Love Mommy!" he'll sign, over and over, throwing in a couple of his best spoken words—*Hi! Hi! Hi!*—for good measure.

I tell you what, this is mighty hard to resist. His head is snuggled against my arm; he doesn't know I'm watching through slitted eyes, just dying to smother him with kisses. I don't think I've ever in my life seen anything sweeter than a toddler signing "love." Finally he'll drift off to sleep. I lie there, listening to his breathing, watching his hands twitch occasionally as he talks in his sleep. By this time, his unborn sister is usually wide awake, and I often wonder how he can sleep through the pummeling she gives his back. I suppose my belly diminishes the force of the impact somewhat.

I think about him, and I think about this baby who will be joining us in the outside world before long. Eleven years ago, when I was pregnant with Jane and people would ask, "Are you hoping for a boy or a girl?" I'd reply with the standard, "I don't care, as long as the baby is healthy." This wasn't exactly true: secretly I was hoping for a girl. Both hopes came true. I delivered a healthy baby girl, and I was so happy, so grateful.

This little girl didn't remain healthy, though. By the time she was Wonderboy's age, she was fighting for her life. The battle against leukemia was grueling and scary. When, nine months after her diagnosis, Scott and I learned we were expecting another child, I uttered that "I don't care what it is, as long as it's healthy" line with even greater fervency. And then, two babies later (first our Rose, then bouncing Beanie), I gave birth to a little boy, and he *wasn't* healthy. He was, to put it bluntly, rather a mess. Thus began the next chapter of the lesson that started during the long months of Jane's illness.

Being entrusted with the care of a child who is not physically perfect can be, yes, painful and scary, but also one of the sweetest, most rewarding experiences a person can have. Do you know how much they teach us, these small, brave, persevering persons? I hadn't begun to grasp the meaning of that whole "Count it all joy" business in the book of James until I met these children. Now I get it, or at least I get a glimpse of it. There is immeasurable joy not just in the overcoming of trials, but even—I know it sounds implausible, but it's true—in each trial itself.

Patience, cheerfulness, courage, determination, persistence—these virtues which require such effort from me are a matter of course for this boy of mine. And so it was for his oldest sister, when she was in the thick of her ordeal. If we learn by example, then I have surely learned a great deal from my children. What riches Wonderboy's "imperfections" have brought to our lives! A new language, yes. But more than that. Watch him work to achieve the magical "all fall down" at the end of Ring-around-the-rosy—see how intently he studies his sisters and with what careful perseverance he attempts to imitate them. He looks at his legs: hey, I can bend them now! It used to be they wouldn't cooperate with his desires. Grinning, he crouches, he squats, he teeters—he plops onto his bottom! He's done it! The cheers ring out; the girls' delight is genuine and very loud. His face, oh his face—now I know what real joy is.

I have heard this truth beautifully articulated by others. The book *Expecting Adam* is one giant love poem on the subject. The authors are not women who sugarcoat or downplay the challenges; but their writing overflows with quiet joy.

Yesterday at naptime, Wonderboy hung in a little longer before sleep overtook him. After running through all the usual mommy-wooing tactics, he apparently decided he'd have better luck petitioning God. Over his head I watched his hands flash through a litany of prayers: the Sign of the Cross, then the names of all the people we God-bless every night, starting with his daddy and running right on through every member of the family to "the poor, the sick, the needy," and finally: the Pope. He just about got me then; the temptation to just eat him up (and therefore demolish any possibility of a nap) was overpowering.

Instead, I lay there doing some praying of my own. The baby inside me kicked and kicked; I felt her foot against her brother's back and realized how much my answer to that old question has changed over the years. Of course I hope, for her sake, that she will be a healthy child. No mother hopes for her children to have to walk a difficult road; it is our nature to want their paths to be as pleasant as possible. But no longer could I say and mean (even if I didn't know the gender of the child): "I don't care what it is as long as it's healthy," with its tacit suggestion that an unhealthy baby means only tragedy and sorrow.

If that wish had come true last time, I wouldn't have my Wonderboy. If this child—or any of my others, for that matter, for Jane is proof that being "born healthy" is no guarantee of perpetual good health—should encounter serious medical difficulties, I know now that no matter how hard the road may be, even if it leads through the depths of Moria, it will carry us through Lothlorien, too. And even in Moria there can be humor and camaraderie and courage and hope among the band of travelers—especially the smallest ones.

Melissa Wiley is a children's book author and the homeschooling mother of six children including her sweet special-needs Wonderboy. She blogs the adventure at Here in the Bonny Glen.

Emerson, Dominic and Reagan Rizzo

Chapter 9

A Change for the Better

by Shannon Rizzo

We were 16 weeks pregnant with our first child when we went for a "routine" ultrasound. The technicians noticed fluid on the baby's brain, holes in his heart and a short femur. They didn't know what all of that meant, so they put us in touch with a high-risk obstetrician and a genetic counselor. We were told that it could be nothing, an infection or something genetic. That same day, we had a level II ultrasound and agreed to amniocentesis. The results, the doctor told us, could take up to two weeks. After these appointments were over, we drove straight to St. Patrick Cathedral in Charlotte, NC, where we were married less than a year earlier. We cried and prayed, asking God to help us make sense of all of the information we had heard, and also to calm our hearts while we waited for the results.

Ten days later, my doctor called me at work to say that our child had Down syndrome. He went on to tell me that he was obligated to inform us that we had only two weeks to decide if we wanted to abort the pregnancy. Fortunately, this was one of the issues Michael and I had discussed—and agreed upon—during marriage preparation. I told the doctor that we would not even consider abortion. When I hung up the phone, I tried to reach my husband. There was no answer. There I was, sitting in my office, in shock and feeling as if I needed to do something. The thought popped into my head to call the bishop.

Now I understood that Bishop William Curlin was a busy man. Did we know him personally? No. We had seen him several times at Mass, as it was his home parish. But the priest who witnessed our marriage had been reassigned to another city, and we needed some serious spiritual direction. The bishop's secretary told me he was unavailable. I explained in detail the purpose of my call. She said she would pray for us, and took my name and phone number. My husband returned my phone call. I told him of our baby's diagnosis, and he said he would leave work immediately and pick me up at my office. When we hung up, the phone rang again. Imagine my surprise when I heard the bishop himself on the line! He wanted to meet with us right away. He talked with us, encouraged us and led us in prayer. He spoke with us about the power of prayer and the Rosary, and asked if we prayed it regularly. We admitted that we did not. When we left, however, we committed to praying the Rosary together every night.

Despite our uplifting meeting with the bishop, we felt shocked, scared, overwhelmed, fearful, ill equipped and sad that our dreams for this baby were not going to unfold as we had planned. We tried to get our hands on every resource available in order to educate ourselves on children with Down syndrome. We contacted our local Down syndrome group and arranged to meet one of the members and her two-year-old daughter. They came to our house, and within minutes we felt that "we can do this!" Little Melissa was beautiful, smart, funny and entertaining. Meeting her in person gave me hope.

My prior knowledge of individuals with Down syndrome was confined to children in my grade school, who were kept out of sight most of the time. I had no recollection of seeing people with Down syndrome in my community. But after receiving the Down syndrome diagnosis, I saw them everywhere. And in sharing our story, people would often say "my sister," "my uncle," "the girl across the street," "my friend's granddaughter," etc... has Down syndrome. There was a world of resources and support for us.

The Rosary helped us in so many ways. It solidified our united front. It deepened our faith. It brought the Gospel to life. We realized that raising a child with Down syndrome was a small challenge compared to the sacrifice Jesus had made for us. We stopped asking God to change our son, but instead asked Him to prepare us. In addition, for the first time in my life, I began receiving the blood of Christ regularly at Mass. I wanted Jesus' blood to run through my body and that of my unborn child. I was certain this would heal the other health issues he had.

For the remainder of my pregnancy we had level II ultrasounds frequently. Doctors were mainly concerned about the fluid on our baby's brain (hydroencephalus) and the holes in his heart. At my last ultrasound, they checked the fluid to see if his head would be too big for me to deliver naturally. They were also looking at the holes in his heart, to determine whether or not they would need to perform surgery after he was born. The fluid was gone and the holes had closed! The doctors were surprised and had no explanation. I look upon the change as a Eucharistic miracle.

On August 10, 1997, our son, Dominic Michael, was born. He was the first grandchild on both sides of our families, so there was much excitement surrounding his birth. Michael and I were grateful for the months God gave us to educate and prepare ourselves, our families and our friends. As a result, I believe that my birth experience was much like that of most first-time moms—we were all anxious and excited to finally meet Dominic! The feast day for St. Dominic is August 8. St. Dominic had a great devotion to the Mother of God, and she used him to inspire others to know and follow the one, true Lord Jesus Christ, through devotion to the Holy Rosary.

The short version of life from then until now: We participated in early therapies, including physical therapy, occupational therapy and speech therapy. We moved to Pennsylvania when Dominic was two because of the excellent services and school options available there for individuals with special needs. We enrolled Dominic in an inclusive pre-school program at age three. At five, he attended Kindergarten at our local parish school, which has an amazing inclusive program for children with special needs. He stayed there for first and second grades, and five years ago he celebrated the sacraments of Reconciliation and First Holy Communion with his peers. That was a joyful occasion I will never forget!

Dominic is now 12 years old. He is in the seventh grade at our local public school. He has plenty of friends and rides the bus. He is happy, loving and kind to all those he meets. He reads, solves math problems, is a whiz on the computer, plays with his Leapster, and loves SpongeBob and his two younger sisters–Reagan, 6, and Emerson, 4. He attends day camp during the summer, loves to swim, plays t-ball, bowls and performs in musical theater for special actors. Overall, he has a happy life.

As for Michael and I, we cannot imagine our life without Dominic. God used him to change who I am for the better! I feel eternally blessed that God chose me to be his mother!

Shannon Rizzo is a married, working mother of three living in Pittsburgh, PA. She can be reached by email at; shannonrizzo@verizon.net.

Michael and Birgitta O'Brien-Constantino

Chapter 10

Michael and Birgitta's Story

by Monica O'Brien

There is a convent of St. Birgitta near our home. I was on retreat there once and asked for her intercession for another child. I promised that if the next one was a girl I would call her Birgitta. Well, I did get pregnant soon thereafter, but instead of a girl, my son Michael joined our family in October 2001. Somehow, I knew in my heart that a little girl was still coming. Michael would pave the way.

About a year earlier, I had miscarried our little Mary Elizabeth at 17 weeks. My husband and I prayed for another child to join AJ, now 15, and Christine, now 11. When I found out I was pregnant again, I was overjoyed. Everything seemed to be going fine, with the exception that I had excess fluid. I had refused all prenatal testing, but did consent to a sonogram. Nothing seemed to be wrong other than the fluid. The pregnancy proceeded normally. I had planned a home birth and soon found myself calling the midwife. I was ready and so was the baby!

It was a quick labor, and before we could even set up the equipment and camera, Michael was on his way into the world. There was so much fluid, and he needed to be suctioned quite a bit. We both seemed fine afterwards and he began nursing. But something wasn't right. He was smaller than my other two and would spit up more than they did. We took him to his pediatrician on Thursday. He had not lost much of his birth weight and appeared to be doing fine. I was still concerned, however, about the amount of spitting up he did. Our pediatrician and I decided I would bring him back for a follow-up on Monday.

That Sunday, I had Michael in the sling while I vacuumed. He was asleep, but I noticed that he seemed very pale. So, I started up the stairs to show him to my husband. By the time I reached the top step, his lips were blue and his skin was ashen. I took him out of the sling, and we laid his limp body on the changing table. My husband revived him while I called the doctor.

Michael came around and started breathing. His color returned, but he was very weak. We took him to the emergency room and met his doctor there. He was put on an IV and stayed the night. I continued to try to nurse him, and he continued to spit up large amounts of milk. The next day, the doctors tried to insert a tube through his nose. It kept coming back out his mouth. They took an X-ray, which showed that he had a tracheoesophageal fistula and an esophageal atresia. Basically, his esophagus was like a sac; it did not connect with his stomach. The tube just curled up and came back out his mouth. With nowhere to go, his stomach had attached itself to his trachea. Somehow, traces of breast milk got through the trachea into his stomach, allowing him to pass his first bowel movement. This delayed detection of the malformation.

Doctors sent us for surgery to the Morgan Stanley Children's Hospital of New York City. Michael had aspirated after spitting up and consequently developed pneumonia, so we had to wait about a week for him to recuperate. The surgery was successful, but genetic testing revealed that Michael has a mosaic form of trisomy 18, also known as Edwards syndrome. This chromosomal disorder is characterized by three, rather than the usual two, chromosomes on the eighteenth pair. It is similar to trisomy 21, or Down syndrome, in this regard. However, many children with trisomy 18 die in utero or shortly after birth. Michael is mosaic, which means that not all of his cells have three of the 18th chromosome. However, he is at risk for Wilm's tumor, a malignant tumor of the kidney. By the time symptoms appear it can be too late. Therefore, Michael has a sonogram every six months to a year.

Children with trisomy 18 can be affected by mental retardation, developmental delays, heart defects, kidney abnormalities, intestinal problems, delayed growth, small jaw, low-set ears, and even clenched hands. Some, like Michael, suffer from tracheal esophageal fistula and esophageal atresia. Trisomy 18 affects only one in 3,000 births. Michael is not your typical textbook child with Edward's syndrome. He has some issues with his digestive system, but is otherwise very healthy. He has had some minor developmental delays but has been catching up quickly to his peers and often holds his own with others the same age. He struggles cognitively and needs extra support with his schooling, but he is coming along and is quite capable. He has a wicked sense of humor and enjoys pretend play often recreating scenes from movies.

There have, of course, been challenges. But God, His Mother and the saints have been with us every step of the way. I have always had a special devotion to the Blessed Mother. In fact, it was through the Rosary and her love that I was able to fully embrace my faith after a struggle. I know without a doubt that Mary has cared for Michael in a special way.

Due to the problems with his esophagus, Michael would often cough. Food would get caught in his throat. And if he had the slightest cold, his cough would sound horrible, like croup. Basically, his saliva would pool and he needed to clear it. He would often cough so hard that he threw up. The mornings were the worst. It would sometimes take him over an hour to clear his esophagus completely.

In my bedroom, I have a picture of the Blessed Mother and one of Christ. They once hung over my grandparents' bed. Michael started asking me to hold the picture of Mary. He wanted to touch it, but he seemed cautious, almost afraid. He told me that she "takes him". Eventually, he was able to explain to me that she came out of the picture at night and hurt him. I was puzzled and very concerned by his comments. I asked him what he meant. We role-played where he would walk by me and he told me to stretch out my arms and pull him to me. I was to wrap my arms around him and hug him. He showed me what she did to him by using his fingertips to pound on my back. He was not afraid of the woman in the picture, just the discomfort he would feel when she "took" him and pounded on his back.

I didn't understand this until I realized Michael had not had one of his morning coughing fits in a very long time. And he has not had one for over a year. I can now imagine the Blessed Mother tapping on his back—almost like we had to do in the hospital: with a bit of force—to clear his mucous during the night so he would wake with no problems. The Blessed Mother was caring for him!

Michael had just started to walk at 18 months old when we received the call about Birgitta. My husband and I had completed a home study with the state for foster care/adoption prior to Michael's birth. Officials were calling about a baby who was to be released from the hospital. She had Down syndrome and suspected fetal alcohol syndrome because she was born with drugs and alcohol in her blood. Due to sepsis, she received a full blood transfusion, and due to respiratory distress was intubated three times in the course of her 11 days of life.

As soon as I got off the phone with the social worker, I picked up the Bible and asked God for guidance. I opened to a random page and pointed. When I looked down, I saw that my finger was on Matthew 18:5. "And who ever receives one child such as this in my name receives me." Matt 18:5 NABRE. Talk about God hitting you over the head with a two-by-four! I called my husband at work and he immediately responded "Yes!"

We were told our home study would be reviewed and they would call us if we were chosen. The next morning we were asked to pick up the baby. It all happened so fast. My sister was visiting, so she stayed with my children while her older daughters came with Michael and me to pick up the baby. Michael was only 18 months old, and I could not yet leave him behind.

On the way home, I called my pastor to tell him that we did it! He knew about the call the previous day, and said that we could have Birgitta baptized right after Mass that Sunday. What a joyous day that was! We were greeted after Mass by many well-wishers. Since things had happened so quickly, they were all surprised to see us with a new baby.

The next year was very difficult. Clerical errors and red tape slowed the adoption process. To make matters more difficult, Birgitta's birth mother's rights were not terminated for almost two years; in the meantime, we were considered to be her foster parents. After the birth mother failed to show up for visitation time and time again, a judge finally terminated her rights. The only thing that got us through all of this was our faith in God and the support of family and friends.

During those first two years of her life, we saw many specialists. We now have a confirmed diagnosis of fetal alcohol syndrome, Down syndrome, sensory integration disorder and, recently, autism.

One of the many blessings we have received through this adoption is watching Michael progress rapidly. We had a slight fear that he might regress with a new baby in the house. Instead, he became an amazing big brother. He moved forward at rapid speed, taking his role as big brother seriously. Birgitta is just a sheer blessing. That is not to say parenting her is not sometimes difficult or hard work, but then, who said being a parent of any child would be easy? Our faith teaches us that life is precious—all life. I believe that God has graced our family with the presence of living angels. How truly blessed we are!

Monica and her family live in Connecticut.

Eileen and Johanna Benthal

Chapter 11

The Path of Miracles

by Eileen Benthal

Miracles do happen. They just don't always look the way we think they're supposed to look. After more than seventy surgeries, my youngest daughter is a testament to the existence of miracles.

Fifteen years ago, Johanna was born with a large mass on her brainstem. At three months of age she had the first of many brain surgeries. The night before doctors were to remove the mass, I sat in a rocking chair with my little girl on my lap. I prayed from the depth of my heart. In the stillness of that dark night, I heard a whisper that I knew was God. "I can take her now and her pain will end," He said, "or she can live now, but it will be a hard road ahead."

The mysterious words prompted an immediate response from the depths of my soul. I wasn't certain if the Author of Life was giving me a say in my daughter's future, but I knew He had already given me a reply.

"I choose the path of miracles!" I shouted in the dark hospital room, breaking the silence and welcoming the dawn of a new day.

Since that time, we've watched many miracles unfold. At eighteen months, doctors finally diagnosed Johanna with multiple cavernous angiomas. Her brain has many of these lesions, which hemorrhage frequently and often require surgery. She also has a shunt in her brain to control fluid pressure. Shunts frequently malfunction, thus causing the need for more brain surgeries. Johanna has endured a hard road, but she is stronger and more beautiful for it. An unmistakable mystery surrounds her and our entire family of four children. We have learned to appreciate life, especially in the darkest moments, the place where miracles happen.

One such miracle stands out among the rest as a dramatic and extremely painful time. Yet I recall this time as the holiest time of my entire life. It was a time when it seemed as though Heaven and earth met in Johanna's hospital room, as she lay there struggling for life.

We had planned to fly from Long Island to Illinois to celebrate Thanksgiving with my husband's family. Johanna was released from the hospital just days before, and her neurosurgeon cleared her to fly with us. Now all we had to do was pack. With Johanna, packing means emergency medical numbers, medical history, and most recent scans of her brain and shunt system. As we packed, a foreboding feeling came over me. I was really concerned that things would not go well. I tried to ignore the feeling, but it wouldn't go away.

After an uneventful flight, we settled in with family and happily greeted relatives we hadn't seen in several years. There were many preparations to make for the holiday. That foreboding feeling pressed in on me, like suffocating heat, threatening to shatter our plans. Then it happened: Johanna's shunt malfunctioned. As the pressure built up in her brain, cerebral spinal fluid leaked from one of the new incisions.

In conversation with her doctor, we decided that the safest thing to do was to bring her home immediately. We agonized over the decision to have my husband, Steve, remain in Illinois with our older children and I return home with Johanna. As hard as it was to part, we knew that our older kids did not need to spend another holiday in the hospital. We kissed tearful goodbyes as Johanna and I boarded the plane home. She rested peacefully in my arms, staring up at me with her beautiful blue eyes. She has such wisdom for a little girl.

After we arrived at the hospital, doctors treated Joanna for infection and operated to relieve the pressure on her brain. As Johanna always does, she found the good in the situation. We planned a Thanksgiving celebration with our hospital friends, and Johanna spoke to my husband, her brother and two sisters, laughing at stories and blowing kisses into the phone. Steve and I shared tearful whispers and tried to imagine the warmth of our embrace as we each faced the cold days apart.

We enjoyed a sweet Thanksgiving feast with other families. But that night Johanna's conditioned worsened, and she took an unexpected turn as the pressure built up in her brain. As her heart rate and respirations plunged, doctors placed her on a respirator to keep her alive and rushed her back to the operating room. I called my husband and cried.

In the waiting room, I was surrounded by friends who sought to comfort me and to pray with me. The conversations drifted as they tried to distract me. I felt like I was in two places at once: my body was in the waiting room, but my spirit and my thoughts were with Johanna in the operating room. All at once, I saw a picture in my mind of Johanna, the operating room and her surgeon's hands. I knew something was going terribly wrong. With that, I told the women in the room that we needed to pray; that something was wrong. All at once, I felt as if I was in that operating room, praying for Johanna and her neurosurgeon. I knew the hand of God was going to move. I just didn't know what direction He would choose.

Minutes later, though it felt like hours, Johanna's surgeon came to see me. Our eyes met from a distance, and we both knew something had happened. He told me that Johanna had experienced a catastrophic event, the hemorrhage of a major artery of the brain. He thought he had lost her. But the bleeding stopped miraculously on its own, and her vitals remained stable. While he did not know for certain the damage this would cause, at least we knew the bleeding had stopped and Johanna was alive. He explained that he needed to place her in a drug-induced coma to give her brain time to heal.

I sobbed as we spoke, holding hands and listening intently. And then I asked Johanna's neurosurgeon if we could pray together, something we had done several times. As I prayed aloud, words flowed like a melody from my soul. It was a bittersweet song, mixed with gratitude for miracles found and moans of pain deeply felt. Where was God? He was right there with us, where two or more gathered. The path of miracles took a new turn.

My next thought was for my husband and children, and the need to expedite their flight home. I found myself praying for Johanna to survive long enough to say goodbye. When they did arrive that evening, Johanna was in a deep coma. Her icy hands were limp, and when I opened her eyelids, cold, blue eyes stared off in the distance. It was hard to believe she was alive. But what else could I do but hope?

The faith of my other three children amazed me. My 15-year-old son knelt by Johanna's ear, held her icy hand and sang her a lullaby. My daughters, 12 and nine at the time, both chattered lovingly to Johanna, telling her of their trip home and making plans for Christmas. Later, they each broke down in my arms. My husband stood quietly by her bedside and kissed his sweet daughter's head. Single tears rolled down his cheeks, but his pained expression did not change. We began our Advent, waiting for the Lord to come.

In the weeks to follow, there was little to do but wait. Friends kept our children busy with preparations for Christmas and frequent visits to the hospital. During the few visits I made home for a few hours, I felt disconnected from the hustle and bustle of the world, and I longed to return to the solace of Johanna and her room. We played soft music and lit a tiny tree. The rhythmic sound of the respirator reminded us that Johanna's life breathed on. But somehow I knew she was in a holy place, somewhere between Heaven and earth. Right there in her hospital bed, I could feel the presence of God. I knew He held her in His arms while we waited.

Those days were tenuous, as the pressure in her brain climbed to dangerous limits and an aneurysm developed at the sight of the arterial bleed. The doctors decided to wake her slowly to see what lay ahead.

The day they woke Johanna and removed the breathing tube, I felt like I couldn't breathe on my own. I feared that she wouldn't be able to either. I watched her struggle to breathe as the doctors cautiously encouraged her, still ready to put her back on the respirator if she couldn't yet breathe on her own. I felt my knees weaken as I stepped away. Then, prompted by the Holy Spirit, I called out, "Johanna, breathe!"

She turned her head toward me, and her dazed, blue eyes met mine. In that moment, she took a deep breath that filled both her lungs and mine. I'll never take breathing for granted again.

The next day, as Johanna learned to breathe on her own again, we prepared for yet another very dangerous surgery. The aneurysm in her artery was growing larger each day. If it were to explode, she would likely die. So the week before Christmas, we were transferred to New York City for an extremely dangerous surgery to close off the blood flow to the aneurysm.

I remember clearly the day of that surgery. It was my birthday. Our friends, doctors, nurses and staff back at the hospital on Long Island, faxed me birthday wishes and promises of prayers for Johanna. As the surgeon operated on the aneurysm, we prayed.

I remembered how, as a child, I always prayed for snow on my birthday. Now I prayed for the Lord to save my daughter. And I lived with a strange dichotomy that gave peace to my soul. During the weeks of Johanna's coma I felt as if she connected us to Eternity. And I knew that it is, indeed, our promised home. So this time, I was completely at peace, knowing that on my birthday Johanna would come home. Either God would place her in my arms or take her to Heaven. Either way, she was home in the arms of the Lord. That was a birthday gift to me.

God saw fit to place Johanna back in my arms to stay with the family that loves her. The recovery—learning to speak and walk and interact again—was slow and precious. We came home from the hospital a few days after Christmas, just in time to celebrate Little Christmas and rejoice in the Epiphany, a word that means "a manifestation of God."

People often assume that I ask God why my daughter and my family have to suffer so much. Honestly, it's not a question I ask. I choose to believe that the Lord uses all things for good (Romans 8:28). A lot of good has come from these tough times. Our family, though worn out from the struggle, is stronger than most, and our children are wiser because they have seen God's power in the midst of suffering. Johanna's neurosurgeon was baptized a Catholic Christian 18 months after that little miracle on the operating room table. He says he couldn't take credit for saving Johanna. God did it.

God manifested Himself that Thanksgiving, Advent and Christmas season. It was for us a milestone along the path of miracles.

Eileen Benthal lives with her husband and four children on Long Island, where she is a columnist for her hometown newspaper. She and Johanna have appeared at "Healthcare for Gunner" press conference on Capitol Hill and were guests on "Fox and Friends" to demonstrate the abilities of their wonderful service dog.

Ryan Barrett

Chapter 12

The World Needs Wildflowers

by Mary Ellen Barrett

On December 16, 1998, I became something I never expected to be. I became the mother of a disabled child. On that day, in a dreary hospital office of a "leading" children's neurologist, my then, 3-year-old son Ryan was formally diagnosed with autism. It is a diagnosis that our brains had come to accept over the previous few months, but our hearts had yet to embrace. Sitting in that office, hearing the word I had been dreading for awhile, I was rattled and heartsick. It barely even registered when the doctor pointed at my large, six months pregnant belly and said quite callously, "It looks like it's too late to do anything about *that* now."

It didn't hit me until I loaded Ryan and Katie into their car seats and settled my large, waddly self in the car. He meant I should not be having this joyously expected third baby. The third baby, now 8 years old, who is endlessly patient and understanding of her older brother's abnormalities. That third baby, who greets each new baby into the family with gentle hands and loving caresses? This is the baby I shouldn't have had?

Well, fortunately there are other neurologists and other hospitals. There have also been other babies. We are now a family of eight children and God has provided Ryan with a group of siblings who take his progress to heart in a way that constantly touches me.

From the beginning, it was just necessary to surrender this parenting of a "special child" to God. My husband and I felt unequipped to deal with the new role that had been thrust upon us, so we decided not to make this journey alone. God had to be our constant companion. He trusted us with this extraordinary child and we had to believe that the Almighty had a plan and that we needed His help to accomplish it. Our faith in God has been more than rewarded, and Ryan is growing to be a gifted and extraordinary person.

In an environment where he is loved by a passel of younger children no matter how oddly he behaves, Ryan has become more than any of the doctors ever considered he could be. He is the object of some hero worship by our twins who love to hear him play the guitar and sing to them. In sharing a day with their brother, patience, fortitude, love, compassion, humility are all part of my children's everyday lives. It is often difficult, but always worth the effort.

Autism is often an ugly thing. The people affected by it are difficult to live with, unreasonable, not affectionate and immensely stubborn. They have odd quirks and weird obsessions. They have a lower than average life expectancy and, therefore, must somehow have provisions made. They are also uncommonly beautiful and often gifted musically, as in Ryan's case, artistically or mechanically. They enhance their families and they make the world a better place. The large amount of autistic people in society will force us all to be more compassionate and less judgmental. Is the child in the grocery store having a tantrum or experiencing pain due to sensory problems? Is the man in church who won't meet your eye rude or unable to do so because his brain is wired differently?

The current trend of prenatal testing in order to discover any imperfections in an infant before it is born has led to the evil of extermination of some of the more beautiful flowers in our garden. When we weed the wildflowers out of the garden in favor of the perfectly cultivated, pure breeds, we diminish the whole garden. When we stop having children because they may not be physically or emotionally perfect we diminish our families, our society and our souls. My other children have a living, breathing means to Heaven right here in their home. Understanding their brother, loving their brother and taking care of him have forced them to think differently about people and to experience the fruits of real compassion on a daily basis.

As the parent of a child with a disability, you are constantly barraged with the propaganda of the anti-life, pro-perfect people movement. "Why would you take the chance of having another like him?" I was once asked at, of all places, a child's birthday party. The fact is that it has never occurred to us to not have more children because one might be disabled. In the same way, it never occurred to us to not have more because one might turn out to have bucked teeth or a large, bulbous nose. We have welcomed each child as the gift and blessing that God intended.

Ryan was chosen for our family by God. He is our escalator to Heaven, and we are grateful for this gift God has given us, this means to acquire virtues we would otherwise not acquire and ultimately gain eternal salvation. I'm not so sure I'd have much of a shot without him.

Mary Ellen Barrett is a columnist for The Long Island Catholic and author of the popular Catholic blog, Tales from the Bonny Blue House.

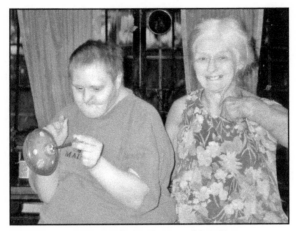

Mary and Tony von Schlegell

Chapter 13

Tony

by Mary von Schlegell

As you, my child, are the limitation
So are you the sweetest consolation of my life
And imitation of our Lord.

Clearer than all in my heart,
Your hands marked with the strange line
Raise, raise my compassion
Cling around my heart.

Oh beautiful, calm face
So small, so quiet beside me,
You have kept me from destruction

Oh how can we ever fathom
The strange economy of a loving God?
Why does our trust so often fail,
With salvation springing even here along our path?

Mary, in her eighties, is caring for her son Tony, in his forties, at home in southern Maine. Tony has Down syndrome. Since he was born before the educational advances which our children enjoy today, the only word he has ever spoken is "Mama."

Kathleen and Julianna Basi

Chapter 14

Not My Plan

by Kathleen M. Basi

"For I know well the plans I have in mind for you—oracle of the LORD—plans
for your welfare and not for woe, so as to give you a future of hope."
Jeremiah 29:11 NABRE

This wasn't how it was supposed to be.

Not that I had a plan--not really. I know better than to tell God how things should be. But the day Julianna was born, I knew this much: things were not the way they were supposed to be.

I was not supposed to be having a repeat C-section. I had controlled my diet throughout pregnancy specifically to avoid it. But at 37 weeks, Julianna somersaulted into a foot-first breech, so off to the O.R. we went.

She was not supposed to be born with low blood sugar. She was not supposed to be whisked off to the nursery for her first feeding, far from the warmth of mother's arms and the nourishment of mother's milk.

My daughter most definitely was not supposed to have Down syndrome. I was not supposed to spend the hours after surgery lying helpless on a hospital bed, while my husband and I wept in each other's arms. We weren't supposed to spend our first hours with our daughter wondering how—or if—she would ever function independently in adulthood.

She wasn't supposed to be born with three holes in her heart, or to have blood drawn six times in the first three days. Nor was she supposed to become so jaundiced that she had to spend those days under bilirubin lights, only visiting me long enough to nurse.

I wasn't supposed to spend two-and-a-half days alone in a hospital room while my husband argued with nurses and doctors by telephone. He wasn't supposed to be fighting medical battles while simultaneously trying to maintain a normal routine for our 2-year-old son, Alex.

We weren't supposed to spend Julianna's first week running from one hospital to another for echocardiograms and genetic counseling, sitting in examining rooms for hours while doctors disrespected our time and Alex began to act out from sheer boredom.

Julianna wasn't supposed to need heart medicine that made her lose a pound in her third week. She wasn't supposed to start her life with the threat of open-heart surgery looming over her.

We weren't supposed to receive an e-mail praying that God would remove the demonic influence from our daughter and make her perfectly healthy.

A lot of things weren't supposed to happen. Or so I thought.

But as time goes by, I am learning that in spite of how wrong everything seemed those first few days, God does have a plan. It's just not my plan.

Julianna *was* supposed to be born into a family that gathered fiercely around her—and us—from the moment the words "chromosomal abnormality" first were spoken. It was God who gave her four grandparents who adored her at first sight, lavishing her with love when her parents were too overwhelmed to do so. It was God who gave her one uncle who would defend her passionately before he even saw her picture and another who has a special place in his heart for children just like her. It was God who surrounded her with aunts who are teachers, physical therapists, lawyers and researchers—to say nothing of the army of cousins waiting in the wings. In other words, it was God who sent Julianna to a family particularly suited to welcome her into this world.

Alex *is* supposed to have a little sister whose very nature will challenge him to be kinder and gentler than he would otherwise have been.

My husband *is* supposed to have a child whose very nature challenges him to release control into God's hands—an act of faith greater than any he has faced before.

I *am* supposed to have a child whose very nature challenges my notion of "perfect," a child who teaches me to recognize the beauty in every person I meet.

I do not know what challenges we will face in the days, months and years to come. I do know that God has a plan, and that in time, He will reveal it. At times, I still grieve for the child I planned to have. But at the same time, I am fiercely in love with this little girl whom God has given into my care. And as she changes me from the woman I am into the woman I am called to be, I pray that God will make me worthy of her love.

Kathleen Basi is a stay-at-home mom, freelance writer, flute and voice teacher, composer, choir director, natural family planning teacher, scrap booker, sometime-chef and budding disability rights activist. She puts her juggling skills on display at www.kathleenbasi.com.

Marie, Nancy and Karen Valko

Chapter 15

The Hospital Visit

by Nancy Valko

I didn't have a plan for this.

It was 1982, and I just stayed awake, crying and smoking five packs a day in my hospital bed after my daughter was born. The fact that Karen had Down syndrome was a shock, but the news that, according to the cardiologist, she only had two weeks to two months to live because of an inoperable heart defect was unbearable.

At the time, I had a 5-year-old son and a 3-year-old daughter excitedly waiting for their new sister and a husband recovering from depression. I was sure we could all adjust to the Down syndrome, but I couldn't imagine any of us capable of watching our baby die. In desperation, I asked the nurses if they knew of anyone who had gone through the death of a child. No one knew of anyone like that, but one nurse did suggest a co-worker who took in foster children. I couldn't understand how that nurse could possibly help, but, as I said, I was desperate.

Anna came in late one night, and I poured my heart out to her. I admitted that I was afraid to get close to my baby because of the pain of losing her and I agonized about letting my other children get too attached to Karen. And, of course, I was worried about my husband's depression spiraling out of control.

Anna told me that every time she gave up a foster child to adoption, it was like a little death to her because that child was gone, possibly forever. Then she told me something surprising. She told me that she could tell I was the kind of person who would automatically give my heart to my child. I remember thinking at the time that she had more faith in me than I had in myself.

Then she told me something I would never forget. Anna said that giving my heart to my child was a no-lose proposition. "If Karen dies, you will have the comfort of knowing that you gave her everything possible, and if she lives you will have the comfort of knowing that you didn't waste any time," she said. Anna also told me to trust God.

Those words were like a healing balm because they were so true and just what I needed. It turned out that the doctors were wrong and three weeks after Karen was born, we found out that her heart defect was indeed operable. Unfortunately, Karen died at 5-and-a-half months from complications of pneumonia and just before her open-heart surgery. But her short, precious life did, indeed, prove the wisdom of Anna's words.

Not long after Karen died, I went back to the hospital to thank Anna for her advice. But even though I had graduated from nursing school at that hospital and knew the nurses there, no one could remember Anna or even anyone like her.

I finally talked to the supervisor; an old friend who came to see me after Karen was born. She was positive that no one like Anna was there at the time but--and this made the hairs on both our necks stand up--she suggested that perhaps Anna was an angel.

Of course, we'll never know for sure. Saint Ann is not only my namesake but also the mother of the Blessed Virgin herself. And I can certainly imagine St. Ann speaking those same words of wisdom to one of her suffering children.

Nancy Valko, RN, a contributing editor for Voices and long-time advocate of patients with disabilities, writes the regular "Bioethics Watch" column for Voices. She is president of Missouri Nurses for Life, a spokesman for the National Association of Pro-life Nurses, a board member of Missouri Right to Life, and past co-chair of the Saint Louis Archdiocesan Pro-Life Committee. She has appeared on many radio and television shows on various medical, ethical, and pro-life topics; and she has written on this topic for The National Catholic Register, the National Right to Life News, the St. Louis Post-Dispatch, First Things magazine and other publications. She and her husband, Kevin Scannell, live in St. Louis, Mo. Together, they have four children and three grandchildren.

Rick Santorum

Chapter 16

Two Years Worth Every Tear

Reprinted with permission from *The Philadelphia Inquirer,* **May 5, 2010**

"Incompatible with life." The doctor's words kept echoing in my head as I held my sobbing wife, Karen, just four days after the birth of our eighth child, Isabella Maria.

Bella was born with three No. 18 chromosomes, rather than the normal two. The statistics were heartbreaking: About 90 percent of

66

children with the disorder, known as trisomy 18, die before or during birth, and 90 percent of those who survive die within the first year.

Bella was baptized that day, and then we spent every waking hour at her bedside, giving her a lifetime's worth of love and care. However, not only did she not die; she came home in just 10 days.

She was sent home on hospice care, strange as that sounded for a newborn. The hospice doctor visited us the next day and described in graphic detail how Bella would die. In sum, she could die at any time without warning, and the best we could hope for was that she would die of the common cold. Karen and I discontinued hospice so that we and our amazing doctors, James Baugh and Sunil Kapoor, could get to work focusing on Bella's health, not her death.

Like so many moms of special kids, Karen is a warrior, caring for Bella night and day and, at times, fighting with health-care providers and our insurance company to get our daughter the care she needs.

Being the parent of a special child gives one exceptional insight into the negative perception of the disabled among many medical professionals, particularly when they see your child as having an intellectual disability. Sadly, we discovered that not only did we have to search for doctors who had experience with trisomy 18. We also had to search for those who saw Bella not as a fatal diagnosis, but as a wanted and loved daughter and sister, as well as a beautiful gift from God.

We knew from experience that Children's Hospital of Philadelphia was such a place. Fourteen years ago, we had another baby who was diagnosed as having no hope, but CHOP's Dr. Scott Adzick gave him a shot at life. In the end, we lost our son Gabriel, but we will always be grateful to Dr. Adzick for affirming the value of his life.

When Bella was 3 months old, she needed some minor but vital surgery. Some doctors told us that a child like Bella wouldn't survive surgery or, even worse, that surgery was "not recommended" because of her genetic condition. In other words, that her life wasn't worth saving. So we again turned to the Children's Hospital and found compassion, concern, and hope in Dr. Thane Blinman. He told us he had several trisomy 18 patients who did well -- and so did Bella.

Next week, we will mark Bella's second birthday. Over these two years, we have endured two close brushes with death, lots of sleepless nights, more than a month in CHOP's intensive care unit, and the constant anxiety that the next day could be our little girl's last.

And yet we have also been inspired -- by her fighting spirit, and by the miracle of seeing our little flower blossom into a loving, joyful child who is at the center of our family life.

Most children with trisomy 18 diagnosed in the womb are aborted. Most who survive birth are given hospice care until they die. In these cases, doctors advise parents that these disabled children will die young or be a burden to them and society. But couldn't the same be said of many healthy children?

All children are gifts that come with no guarantees. While Bella's life may not be long, and though she requires our constant care, she is worth every tear.

Living with Bella has been a course in character and virtue. She makes us better. And it's not just our family; she enriches every life she touches. In the end, isn't that what every parent hopes for his or her child?

Happy birthday, Isabella!

Rick Santorum is a senior fellow at the Ethics & Public Policy Center and former U.S. Senator (R-PA). He is currently a candidate for president.

Dr. Judith Mascolo and Christina Anne Le

Chapter 17

A Doctor's Story

Dr. Judith Mascolo

Becoming a mother of three daughters changed my life. Becoming Christina Anne's mother saved my soul. While I am a pro-life doctor today, my journey to this point has been long and circuitous.

I have been practicing medicine for 16 years. I am a product of the post-Roe v. Wade years. Although I am a graduate of Holy Cross College, I am sad to admit that my Catholic faith was not strengthened or nurtured there to any extent. I actually came close to losing my faith there, if not for a week-long retreat based on the Spiritual Exercises of St. Ignatius of Loyola I made my senior year. By the time I graduated from college I was more of a believer in moral relativism than of Catholic morality. I spent most of the next two decades denying the existence of evil and sin.

It was with this mindset that I entered medical school. God faded into the background as science and technology took preeminence. It didn't take me long to realize that I was surrounded by a lot of pro-abortion people. I was never pro-abortion, but I felt intimidated and ill-equipped to defend the pro-life position. In that class of about 100 students, there were only three or four of us who were pro-life.

I did not know it at the time, but God was about to guide me through a series of events and encounters that would lead me back to the Church. This journey took almost 20 years, finally crystallizing for me in 2005. I want to share with you some of the things I experienced during this journey.

During my last year of residency, I was pregnant with my first child. The timing wasn't great; I was about to embark on my career. I knew a baby would delay so much of what I had been working toward for the last decade. As my colleagues traveled around the country interviewing for jobs, I stayed home preparing for the birth. I was happy to be pregnant, but still a little conflicted by it all. I think some of my fellow residents picked up on this. One day I came into my office and discovered on my desk that someone left me brochures for abortion services from the local Planned Parenthood clinic. The message was clear. I wondered what kind of doctors my colleagues were if they could so easily recommend destroying a life because it didn't fit into their plans.

A couple of years later, when I was pregnant with my second child, I went through the usual prenatal screening tests because I was an older mother and blindly followed my doctor's advice. A blood test indicated that the baby had a very high chance of being born with a chromosomal defect. I remember receiving this news with my husband, my doctor and the genetic counselor. The counselor told us that the abnormality, at its worst, would be incompatible with life. At best, the baby would be born alive, but would probably not survive its first year of life. She urged me to consider an abortion. She said the staff was prepared to do an amniocentesis right then to confirm the diagnosis. We agreed to it and then went home to wait for the results. Now, 15 years later, I can tell you that my daughter is a perfectly healthy, vibrant young lady!

I tell you these two stories to illustrate how easily abortion has crept into and overtaken the soul of medicine—just as Pope Paul VI predicted it would in his encyclical *Humanae Vitae*. If the pregnancy is inconvenient or the baby not perfect, get rid of it!

God was not finished with me yet. He had an even bigger test for me to endure. A few years later, I became pregnant a third time, but this ended in an early miscarriage. Shortly after that, I became pregnant a fourth time. By this time, I was in my early 40s and I knew the risks. I had the prenatal blood test, and, once again, it came back abnormal. I wasn't worried; I had been down this road before. Again, I decided to have the amniocentesis. I thought that I was going to prove to the doctors that there was nothing wrong.

God, however, had other plans. Two days before Christmas, my midwife called and said, "The amnio results confirmed that the baby has Down syndrome." She said that if I wanted an abortion, I needed to make an appointment the following week: just like that, as if I was scheduling a root canal or something.

I took the news hard. My faith in God was not yet on firm ground, and I couldn't understand why this was happening to our family. I felt abandoned. Now I know that when you feel abandoned by God, He has not left your life, but is actually drawing you closer to Him through your suffering. For some of us, He may make His presence known in not-so-subtle ways. For me, He led me to experience things that could not be described as mere coincidences. For the next two weeks, it seemed that everywhere I looked, I saw someone with Down syndrome. They were on television shows, acting in dramas, and working in supermarkets bagging my groceries. One little girl came to me as a patient. Her mother was so happy to tell me about how Rose had come into her life and changed her family in so many wonderful ways.

The most direct way God reached out to me was during Christmas Mass just two days after I received the news. My family decided to attend Mass in my hometown that Christmas morning, a church I had not visited for years. Father Cody celebrated the Mass and gave the homily that day. He spoke about a young family whose baby daughter he had recently baptized. She has Down syndrome. He spoke about the courage of these parents, who when faced with their daughter's diagnosis before her birth, resisted the pressure of their own parents, family, friends and doctors to abort their baby. Instead, they chose life for her. Their pregnancy, the birth of their daughter, and the heart surgeries this baby endured in the early months of her life were all chronicled in a series of articles in the *Boston Globe* and then published into a book titled, *Choosing Naia*. Later, a documentary on 20/20 chronicled the family's experiences. This family trusted God and chose life, even when almost everyone in their lives urged them to terminate the pregnancy and move on.

As I sat there listening to Father Cody, I felt a sudden peace overtake me. I knew that whatever happened, God had His hand in it. I won't tell you that the rest of the pregnancy was easy. Fears and doubts plagued me as the culture of death tried to wear me down. It seems that almost everyone had an opinion about what we should do with this baby, and none of it was acceptable.

To anyone who thinks eugenics is not practiced in this country, consider this statistic: nine out of 10 babies diagnosed prenatally with Down syndrome are aborted. In 2007, the American College of Obstetricians and Gynecologists announced that they would like to see this increase to 100 percent by calling for prenatal screening of Down syndrome for all women in the first trimester, regardless of maternal age. And it won't end with Down syndrome. There will be tests coming soon for all genetic conditions. The American College of Obstetricians and Gynecologists are in a "search and destroy" mode, and for the most part, this is going unchecked by other physician specialties, our society, and the government.

We welcomed our third daughter, Christina Anne, into our family more than ten years ago. She is a joy, and her presence has taken me places I never anticipated. The most important of these is to a closer relationship with Christ. When I finally invited Christ into my professional life, I had no idea at the time of the challenges I would face.

A few years after she was born, I started refusing to write prescriptions for Plan B. I also began warning women that the STDs they have can cause them to be infertile. I talked to my patients about abstinence and chastity. I refused to refer patients to abortion providers. I certainly wasn't yet 100 percent pro-life in my practice of medicine—that would come years later—but I was starting to make some changes and learning to speak up more often. When I commented to our head nurse that a patient who had just received a referral for her 13th abortion could be considered a serial killer, I lost my job.

So there I was the unemployed breadwinner of my family of five and a Catholic doctor with a growing conscience. I knew that my views probably made me unemployable. I could no longer step back into the practice of medicine which was infused with the culture of death. I could no longer sell my soul to the devil. I was given the gift of tangible evidence of the sanctity of life, and I could no longer be silenced!

I had experienced how the culture of death coerces women to choose abortion, not once, but three times with my own pregnancies. I knew it was time for me to commit myself completely to practicing pro-life medicine. My only option was to open my own practice, but I felt so beaten down and so powerless by the system at that point.

However, in the spring of 2005 something happened to me that changed my outlook. This was when Terri Schiavo was murdered and Pope John Paul II died. A few weeks later, I read a pro-life quote in the parish bulletin. It was by Pope John Paul II who said "...the primary goal of all medicine—the service of human life." Well, I felt I had just been hit over the head with a two-by-four! I understood the call of service. After all, I had made the Spiritual Exercises of St. Ignatius of Loyola many years before at College of the Holy Cross, and service to others was ingrained in us by Father LaBran. And, of course, medicine was all about caring for human life. But where and when did it all go so wrong?

That quote, along with the deaths of Terri Schiavo and Pope John Paul II, were the catalysts I needed to make sense of my past experiences—the tests and trials I went through. I made the decision that going forward, I would be a truly pro-life doctor, and I would place my trust in Christ and go where He tells me to go.

I never dreamed how revolutionary that idea would be. I have met other pro-life doctors; some are open about it, others do not feel ready to go public because of their work situation. I was lucky. It was my youngest daughter; the one so many people thought we should just "get rid of," who gave me the courage to live out my conviction to be a truly Catholic doctor. I realize that my role as a doctor and a mother of a disabled child gives me a unique platform to speak out in defense of life. My daughter forced me to look at the world differently. Life at all stages and all abilities is sacred though it is unbelievable to see how this concept is shunned by the rest of the world. As a mother of three girls, I also realize that I have to be the type of doctor I would want for my daughters.

I know, from my own personal experience that doctors are suffering from the misery they encounter every day because of the damage brought about by contraception, divorce, adultery, abortion, promiscuity, teenage pregnancy, poverty, pornography and domestic violence. We see it in the high rates of depression, anxiety, alcoholism, drug addiction, sexually transmitted diseases and infertility in our patients. And I know that most doctors feel powerless to do anything to change the downward trajectory on which the world seems to be heading.

I certainly felt that way before I launched my solo practice in 2007. Some colleagues, in fact, told me that I would never succeed if I refused to prescribe birth control, or refer women for abortions, sterilizations or IVF. And yet today, the practice is six years old, and I am as busy as ever. Patients come to me from nearby states because there are no pro-life doctors in their states. Mothers ask me to see their teen-age daughters because they know I won't put their daughters on birth control pills. Many young couples come to me because I fully support natural family planning.

I used to think that I was the only pro-life physician in Connecticut. In the past four years, I have spoken frequently about my journey back to the Church and how I have brought my faith into my practice of medicine. Many times, after hearing my talk, people approach me and say, "My doctor is Catholic and I think he is also pro-life, but he works in a group of other doctors and cannot practice like you do."

Since launching my practice, I had dreamed about starting a local chapter of the Catholic Medical Association. Catholic doctors need an organization where they can find spiritual and professional support, and for the past 100 years, the CMA has been providing just that. In the fall of 2010, I met another person who also had this dream, and together, Deacon Tom Davis and I met with several doctors, a dentist and a medical student on April 3, 2011 to organize the first Connecticut Guild of the

CMA. Another six physicians in Connecticut have expressed interest in joining the Guild. I am confident that this organization will grow as we get the word out to more doctors. I believe that the CMA has an essential role in defeating the culture of death in the medical profession.

Christina Anne will probably never understand the profound effect she has had on my life, but that's alright. I'm just so grateful that she and her sisters are part of my life, and that with each pregnancy, I chose life.

Dr. Mascolo and her husband live with their three daughters in Connecticut, where she has a solo practice as a general practitioner and is in demand as a pro-life speaker.

Mark O'Friel

Chapter 18

A Journey in Faith through RISEN

by Jane O'Friel, RN

I am a registered nurse, but it was the birth of my son with Down syndrome that changed my life completely. Because of Mark, I became an innovator in the field of Catholic education and my husband and I experienced a renewal of our Catholic faith. Thanks to him, our family and dozens of others in our community have been enriched. Who could have anticipated that my infant son could work so many changes in so many people?

The birth of my second child, Mark, while complicated during the last trimester, was uneventful. Arriving home with my beautiful son, I was filled with hope and love. During the first month following Mark's birth, I noticed that he seemed sluggish and that I had to actually wake him up for feedings. Finding this a bit unusual, I had questions when I went to his first month appointment with the pediatrician. The doctor ordered a chromosome analysis to rule out the possibility of an abnormality. Given that Mark had few outward signs of trisomy 21, I was sure that this test would come back negative. However, the reality was quite different than I expected.

Devastated by the news, my husband and I were able to find many resources to help us cope with the stunning news of Mark's Down syndrome. One of them was our own aunt, a Daughter of Charity who had been the Director of the Kennedy Center for children with developmental disabilities in the Archdiocese of New York. With this spiritual and intellectual support, we were able to connect to the therapists and specialists that are so necessary during the first years of life. Our faith helped hold us together and care for Mark, doing the same things that we were doing for our older child.

As I was considering the possibilities of education for my now 3-year-old with Down syndrome, I reflected on the fact that an inclusive faith-based setting would have so many benefits for my child. My older son, Zachary, was already enrolled in a Catholic school. The mission and vision of the Catholic school seemed to embrace of all of God's children.

Respect for life in its truest sense means more than protection of the unborn. There is a lifetime of joys, challenges and struggles that an individual encounters when faced with a disability. The energies exerted so worthily to protect the unborn need to continue throughout the person's life. And so, I started on my journey.

After a great deal of research within the Catholic church and school network, I found that there was more activity to support this mission than I had thought. There were several documents supporting this effort, most important being the Scriptures themselves. Now we are in the midst of the tenth academic year of R.I.S.E.N. (Responding to Inclusive Special Education Needs) in the Diocese of Norwich, CT. It has been a very interesting and enriching experience.

After many years of being away from the sacrament of Reconciliation, all of a sudden this became a very important part of my life. Ironically, at the same time, my husband was experiencing the same journey. I also started to reflect upon the Eucharist and became profoundly open to what I seemed to have missed for so many years. My experience during adoration of the Blessed Sacrament was bringing back memories of younger years, when I saw religious men and women immersed in the benefits of this most precious time.

So, as I continued to take myself through the planning stages of the R.I.S.E.N. program, I became more profoundly spiritual. My eyes, my mind, my soul and my heart were opened up to the influence of the Most Sacred Heart of Jesus and the Immaculate Heart of Mary. I began to read about the lives of the saints, and to reflect upon their pearls of wisdom and those of the Holy Spirit who clarifies current events. With this firm foundation, I was able to present the idea of including those with special needs in the Catholic community with a perspective that truly reflected the Scripture. I became involved in the Diocese researching sacramental issues for persons with disabilities. And, of course, closest to my heart was the inclusion of children with special needs within the Catholic schools.

The R.I.S.E.N. program should be offered by all Catholic schools. However, the stumbling blocks are frustrating, and I understand how they can even make one consider drifting from the Catholic church. In fact, I did see that happening to those around me. On a positive note, there are many opportunities that can be opened for persons with disabilities, if only we believe and persist in our efforts.

The major areas of consideration when developing an initiative for children with disabilities include social, ethical, legal, political, educational, spiritual and philosophical issues, and the financial stability of a program. Due to circumstances beyond our control, the access to support services (physical therapy, speech and occupational therapy) available through the public sector is a challenge. This is a major ethical issue, as most of the disabilities are of medical nature, for which the crossover between church and state causes difficulties. Lack of support poses a particular stumbling block as the children need the strongest curriculum possible. Through the efforts of the R.I.S.E.N. program, we have been successful in establishing a resource room staffed with a special education teacher and assistants. Over 40 students in Sacred Heart Catholic School utilize the resource room during the day, enhancing their inclusion in the typical classroom setting. The number of students assisted varies from year to year and encompasses direct classroom assistance and an enrichment program. Speech, occupational and physical therapists are coordinated through the local public school, in response to the child's Individualized Service Plan, come once a week to give one-on-one therapy to the students.

Spreading the word about the special needs program is paramount, as you need to obtain community support and sound advice in order to accomplish your goals. The entire grant writing and fundraising piece has to be sound and include reliable volunteers willing to promote the program if it is to be successful. This may require the hiring of personnel to accomplish this important task. Another important issue is professional development of staff. It is essential that faculty are educated in strategies to promote inclusion in the educational setting, and that they attend workshops to develop more knowledge and ideas.

In short, the creation and implementation of programs to assist persons with disabilities requires dedication, commitment, initiative, creativity and love. Faith is the cornerstone through which all things flow. So in my experience, all things are possible with God, and it is through the grace of the Holy Spirit that the most amazing things can happen. I owe this entire project to my supportive family and my amazing son Mark, who graduated eighth grade in 2010, and is recently registered in high school supportive of inclusive practices for persons with disabilities.

Jane O'Friel is a registered nurse, diabetes educator, and founding parent of the RISEN Program of Sacred Heart School, Groton. She continues with her passion for Inclusive Catholic Education as a Consultant to the RISEN Program. She lives with her two sons in the Diocese of Norwich, Connecticut.

Christina and Andrew Bogdan

Chapter 19

Choosing Life

by Christina Bogdan

Let the children come to me; do not prevent them, for the kingdom
of God belongs to such as these. (Mark 10:14-16 NABRE)

I have always been afraid of the unknown. When the phone call came
that late winter morning, the unknown engulfed me. My doctor on the
other end was explaining that the blood test showed that there was a
possibility that my unborn child could have Down syndrome. How could
that be? I already had six completely healthy children. I was only thirty
three years old. So our journey began, not knowing the outcome. Not
knowing the splendid *gift* God had in-store for us.

Our prayer began... "Trust in the LORD with all your heart, on your
own intelligence do not rely; In all your ways be mindful of him, and
he will make straight your paths." Proverbs 3:5 NABRE. Then testing
started with ultrasounds to observe the thickness of our son's neck and
the proportions of his tiny limbs. The results were inconclusive. Then the

fetal eco-cardiogram looked good, but still the doctor sent me to a genetic counselor. I had never heard of genetic counseling. My husband and I sat nervously in the waiting room, while people filed in and out. Next it was our turn. We really weren't acquainted with Down syndrome at all. I never heard one positive thing about children or adults with Downs from the genetic counselors. Looking back, I believe that they really don't have all the facts. They are either ignorant by choice or by neglect.

After a few very stressful months, the day finally arrived. It was a very warm late summer afternoon. We had had a false alarm a few days before and this day, a Monday was to be *Labor Day*. As soon as little Andrew was born I was able to hold him, and I knew immediately that he had Down syndrome. The doctor and nurses quickly whisked him away and more testing ensued. We had a rough few weeks early on, with a bout of jaundice and a second hospital stay, but overall, Andrew is blessed with very good health.

Each of our ten children is a blessing from God, for which I thank Him each and every day. But Andrew is a blessing to everyone who meets him. When he smiles, you can't help but smile back. My husband, Thom says that looking into Andrew's face is like looking into the face of God. Andrew has inspired his oldest sister, Mary to pursue special education in college.

At first I was so worried about the unknown, until a friend told us that God sent Andrew to the right family. Of course He did. Why would I ever think otherwise? With a 92% abortion rate for babies diagnosed with Down syndrome, and new specialized testing available to test even earlier in the pregnancy, I know now that God has a task for all of us: to tell the world what a blessing children with Down syndrome are. All life that God has created is sacred, and it is our job to bring the truth to everyone who crosses our path.

Christina Bogdan lives with her husband and children in Pennsylvania. She writes for her diocesan newspaper, "The Philadelphia Standard and Times". She can be reached at mommychristina@msn.com

Leticia and Christina Velasquez

Chapter 20

A Special Mother is Born

by Leticia Velasquez

"**G**od would never send us a special child," I mused, caressing my pregnant belly, "our marriage isn't strong enough."

I was deliriously happy to be pregnant at 39, for three of my five pregnancies had ended in miscarriage, and my younger daughter, Isabella, was an independent four year old. The summer before, I had returned from a homeschool conference with an aching heart, longing for a translucent-skinned newborn nuzzling my neck.

When my pregnancy lasted past my danger zone, I was ecstatic, and refused the triple-screen blood test.

"There's nothing you can tell me that will make me end my baby's life," I told my doctor, putting the subject of prenatal diagnosis to rest.

Or so I thought.

Five months along, I was attending Sunday Mass, absent-mindedly watching the parishioners with Down syndrome from a local group home when, from out of the blue, I heard an internal voice: "You're going to have a child with Down syndrome."

Astounded, I tried to dismiss it as a hormonal fixation, until, in line for Communion, the voice spoke again: "I want you to accept this child as a gift from My Hand, when you receive Me."

Now I knew there was no escape. Jesus had a call for my life. How would I respond? I choked, "Yes, Lord, as long as you bring my husband along for the ride." I received His Body in tears.

My husband, Francisco, was floored, thinking that I had finally gone over the edge. I also began to doubt the message, since there had been so many normal sonograms.

"And besides, Lord, I've seen these mothers of special children. They're saints. You could NEVER compare my impetuous personality with theirs."

That, I decided, was the clincher. God gave special children to saintly women. I was safe.

Never tell God what He is capable of doing. During the remaining months, I struggled with self-pity, and even, for one instant, regretted my pregnancy.

Two days after the incident at Mass, Fr. Frank Pavone's EWTN Show "Defending Life" featured a pair of sisters, the younger of whom had Down syndrome. Her older sister described her as a blessing for the family: She worked all day, attended daily Mass, prayed the Rosary, and whenever there was a family conflict, she was the one who brought about reconciliation. She ended the show singing a love song she had composed for Jesus. I saw this as a confirmation that I had indeed heard from Jesus at Mass, and that His grace was molding my heart.

The time came for little Christina Maria's arrival. At her birth, the delivery room fell deathly silent. Alarmed, I glanced over at the pink, wriggling baby in the isolette, and asked "What's the problem?" The doctor didn't respond. Francisco tried to tell me in Spanish that Christina was a "mongolita" (Spanish for mongoloid), but I didn't understand. So, on the way to my room, the nurses circled my gurney and said coldly, "We regret to tell you that this child has symptoms consistent with Down syndrome."

I was ready with my response. "This child will never take drugs, go Goth, or shoot up a schoolroom. She'll learn the Faith and keep it her whole life. She's my best chance at getting a daughter to Heaven, and I consider her a special blessing from God." My answer came from a book, *Pregnancy Diary*, by Mary Arnold, which I had read regularly for inspiration.

But words are cheap. What cost me dearly was watching the other newborns in the nursery and comparing Christina's weakness to their vitality. I resented the happy chatter of the other Moms in the ward. I was haunted by dark thoughts, and self-pity took hold of me.

Just then, the phone calls began. My mother and homeschooling friends had summoned support from around the country, and I was encircled in love. I spoke with Marie, a mother from my parish who answered many of my anxious questions and told me what it was like to raise her youngest daughter with Down syndrome. Katie was 20, a high school graduate who walked to work in a local bakery, was godmother to three of her nieces, and was planning an enormous 21st birthday party. Another friend, the mother of 11, sent an Elizabeth Ministry package for special babies, with a CD and book set titled, *Sometimes Miracles Hide, Stirring Letters from Those Who Discovered God's Blessings in a Special Child*, by Bruce Carroll. That book was a constant companion, reminding me that regardless of how inadequate I felt, God had, indeed, chosen me to mother Christina, and that she would be my means of attaining holiness down the road. God's favorite road, the Via Dolorosa.

On Mother's Day, the day of Christina's Baptism, we shared that song with the over 100 guests who crowded the church. My heart swelled with gratitude to God for choosing my family to raise Christina. And when her godmother asked what she should pray for, I didn't ask for a cure from

Down syndrome. I was beginning to understand that her "condition" was a blessing, not a curse. Perhaps, as Fr. McCartney had said, Christina pities us for not having the purity of heart to see what she sees.

Francisco still had to journey towards accepting Christina's diagnosis. When she was first born, he had difficulty holding her, and asked if we could avoid having mail with the words "Down syndrome" arrive at the house. He wanted no part in her care. I was devastated. Thankfully, two men—my father and a friend from a prayer group—took it upon themselves to approach Francisco quietly and remind him that he, too, had been chosen by Our Lord to raise Christina. He began to hold her, and little by little, she wound her way into his heart. The next step involved taking Christina out in public. I worked on Saturdays, leaving him home with three girls, and soon, he began to take them on walks into town and bike rides to the beach. We attended a Spanish language parent support group at a local church, and the example of macho Latino dads publicly sporting their children with Down syndrome on their shoulders, was a powerful example of a father's unconditional love a reflection of God the Father's love for us. Now, Christina is the apple of his eye, and they are inseparable. I watch them with joy as, hand in hand, they pick corn in the garden, or examine a dragonfly in the river, then practice skipping stones. Through prayer, good example and counsel from holy men, God helped my husband see his indispensible role in raising his precious daughter.

After years of specialists, therapists and conferences, our family has grown in acceptance of Christina's halting development, yet often, we are awed by Christina's perception of that which escapes us. One day, I brought her with me to Eucharistic adoration. Entering the chapel, she waved enthusiastically to the monstrance and called, "Hi, Jesus!" I was congratulating myself for having communicated that Jesus was present, though unseen. She promptly put me in my place, for, as we were leaving, she waved again, saying, "Bye Jesus!" as if He was as visible as Grandpa standing in front of her! You know, I believe she did see Jesus. And, what's more, they already had a friendship.

The next stage of growth in special motherhood was to learn to trust Jesus to care for Christina when she was out of my sight. When Christina entered Kindergarten, I was full of anxiety. I wondered how she would fare in a full-day Kindergarten class. Would she make friends? Would she bother the other children, pushing them, stealing their snacks, or knocking down their block towers when they failed to understand her limited language? Would she be left behind the fast-moving curriculum? Would she be frightened and overwhelmed? Christina already knew her numbers and letters, but had difficulty drawing circles and cutting with scissors. She had been trying to master these pre-writing skills for three years with little success. I was secretly afraid that she had hit a plateau with her communication skills.

September and October passed, and we noticed new words entering her vocabulary. In November, her teachers requested a conference before Thanksgiving. It seemed that Christina had exceeded everyone's expectations, and we had to set higher goals for her. She had many friends in school that included her in their daily game of obstacle course on the playground. She was also learning to respect her new friends' block tower creations, to draw circles and to use scissors. I was thrilled. Christina had also given something to Mrs. Brown, her aide at school. In her Christmas note, Mrs. Brown wrote, "Christina has truly brought new meaning to my life. I have learned so much knowing her." This was proof that Jesus was at her side, protecting her so she could flourish, while allowing others to see His presence in her.

I was realizing how much Christina was a gift from the Hand of God to her family, and her community, and that she is a gift we are called to share. In the past five years, we have reached out to families who are expecting children with Down syndrome through my writing and speaking. We have been the subject of articles, and been interviewed on radio and TV, while sharing the joy that people with Down syndrome bring to a family. I have begun my long delayed writing career, motivated by the fact that 92 percent of babies like Christina are aborted. We feel strongly that if expectant families could meet children like Christina, that their hearts would find the courage to welcome their babies into their families as we did.

When she was 12, her sister Gabriela wrote this story about life with her sister with Down syndrome for the diocesan Respect Life essay contest. It won first prize, and has been reprinted many times in various papers and websites. It's called,

"My Sister is Special"

"I have a three year old sister named Christina with Down syndrome. It can be a challenge having a sister with a disability. When she was born, I cried because I knew people would make fun of the way she looked and spoke. Sometimes people give her weird looks as they pass by, but it does not bother me anymore. Those people don't know her like I do. Christina is slow at learning to speak, and I don't always understand her, but that does not stop her from communicating. She says 'let's go' and takes me by the hand to show me what she wants like something to eat or her favorite DVD, and she always says, 'thank you' after you give it to her. Christina didn't learn to walk until she was two and a half, but now you can't stop her! Sometimes, she climbs up on the kitchen island, knocks everything down, and yells for me to come and see her standing up there, with a big smile on her face. She loves running away from me when she is in trouble, giggling.

People with Down syndrome really love, and once in a while, they teach us how to live our faith better. Christina always seems to have a smile on her face, and really cares for others. One time my Mom took Christina to Eucharistic Adoration. As they went into the chapel, she enthusiastically waved and said, 'Hi Jesus!' as if He were standing right in front of her. Everyone in the chapel turned and smiled at her saying, 'she knows He is here.'

Christina is like any other kid, just slower at learning things and she should not be treated differently. Most people don't know that 92% of Down syndrome babies are aborted. The people who do this don't know what they are missing! Every year, my family and I go to Washington D.C. for the March for Life and try to stop this discrimination against unborn babies. Just because they don't have a voice, does not mean their lives should be ended. We have to be their voice. I think nobody

should be rejected because of the way they look or speak.
We are all God's children and He loves all of us."

When Gabbi read her essay to a crowd of 800 and received a standing ovation, I began to see how my vocation to special motherhood involved our entire family, bringing out the best qualities in each member. This challenge was accepted at first reluctantly, then as we each grew to embrace the challenge we grew more patient, more tolerant of the faults of others, and our spiritual life deepened as our priorities were reordered.

We have learned to take time to listen and help Christina learn at her own pace, and cooperate in family activities despite her stubborn streak. Francisco has patiently taught Christina her letters, using a website on the computer. His father Antonio, took her by the hands and taught her to walk, and built countless Lego block towers with her. My parents babysat for her with extraordinary patience and cheered on her accomplishments at school and home. My older daughters regularly help Christina dress for school, do her homework, brush her teeth, and get ready for bed. We have all learned to be slower to judge others by their appearances or abilities, and more likely to look into the souls of those we meet. We have been realizing that the goal of our life as a family is to get each other to Heaven, and that we just may have an advantage because God has given us Christina.

When my daughter Bella was 12, she wrote this poem about Christina:

These children are....
ADorable
LOving
Our Way to Heaven
UNderestimated

Smiley
Young-spirited
UNforgettable
Difficult
Radiant
GOd's miracle
A Mother's joy
An Extra grace to those who need them most.

I continue to share the story of our life with Christina through my blog Cause of Our Joy and it has introduced me to various contributors to this book. In the fall of 2008, with my friend Eileen Haupt, I started Keep Infants with Down Syndrome. KIDS has as its goal the education of society about the abilities of children with Down syndrome and the joy they bring their families and friends, in order to overcome the tragic 92 percent abortion rate of babies with Down syndrome.

Eileen and I met each other and our KIDS members on the morning of January 22, 2009, in 2010, and again this year on Jan 22, 2011, at the National Right to Life Headquarters in Washington DC. We proudly marched in the March for Life alongside our children to the cheers of pro-life onlookers. We gave awards to congressmen who have sponsored legislation to help protect the right to life of children with prenatally diagnosed conditions. We have a special relationship with Rep. Cathy McMorris Rodgers whose son, Cole, has Down syndrome, and inspired his mother to co-found the Congressional Down Syndrome Caucus. KIDS has a blog and a Facebook group, and is growing every day, as those who love someone with Down syndrome are learning that their numbers are dwindling thanks to the pressure women are under to abort their child once trisomy 21 is diagnosed.

Christina, by just being her loving, challenging, fascinating self, has helped me mature spiritually. The virtues of patience, tolerance, and humility are increasing as I learn from the example of a child who communicates with God in ways I will only understand in Heaven. My pastor, says, "suffering, united with humility is the most powerful force on earth." Before I gave birth to Christina, such wisdom would have eluded me, but the humility gained by having to learn such lessons as toilet training over a period of five years instead of one, and having a daughter who does not always fit into society's expectations have taught me the value of patience and finding joy in the smallest of gains, helping our family move towards total surrender of our lives to our loving God.

I have been fortunate to know holy priests and to enjoy the guidance of Blessed John Paul II. I had the honor of attending two events in New York City with him; as a youth in 1979 and as a new mother in 1995. His teaching shaped my vocation as a mother. Here is a meditation of his which has helped me understand my vocation as a special mother.

"The sick, the elderly, the handicapped, and the dying, teach us that our weakness is a creative part of human living, and that suffering can be embraced with no loss of dignity. Without the presence of those people in our midst, we might be tempted to think of health, strength, and power as the only important values to be pursued in life. But the wisdom of Christ and the power of Christ are to be seen in the weakness of those who share his sufferings."

When I was covering the Papal Youth Rally with Pope Benedict XVI for the *National Catholic Register* in April 2008, I was witness to a special moment of grace. Before meeting the 20,000 youth who awaited him outdoors, Pope Benedict conducted a prayer service in the Seminary Chapel, with children with special needs and their families, while we watched on the television screens outdoors. A lovely young lady of 10 who had Down syndrome walked up to the Holy Father to present him with a book. With an outpouring of love so typical of people with Down syndrome, she reached up and hugged him tightly. Not content with their embrace, she turned to the young lady who was at her side, and included her in a three way bear hug.

Tears rolled down my cheeks when I saw the love in the Holy Father's eyes and wondered if he was thinking about his own cousin with Down syndrome. In 1941, this young man was just a few months younger than Josef Ratzinger when he was forcibly taken from his home by the Nazis as part of the T4 Program. German parents at first voluntarily surrendered disabled children for the 'good of the state.' Soon the children were taken against their parents' will. It was the disabled and mentally ill who were the first to experience the horrors of the gas chambers. The boy's family received word a few months later that their son had died. This must have left an indelible impression on the young Josef.

In the past year, I was to learn the power of embracing suffering. And Christina was the one who taught me. My mother was diagnosed with terminal cancer, shortly after Mother's Day of 2009. I wrote "The Prayers of a Little Saint" for Catholic Mom.com.

> We have been dealing with the news that my mother has a malignant tumor. It has been terrifying, yet moments of grace have kept us going. Like when I hear from friends and strangers who are praying for Mom or the look of compassion on my pastor's face when I told him. He lost his mother a few months earlier.
>
> Yesterday God gave us another moment of grace.
>
> I was outdoors with Christina, trying to absorb the gravity of the bad news I had just received by phone: the surgeon said that Mom's cancer was stage four and inoperable. I was trying to move beyond the paralysis of fear and find the words to pray about it. I was trying to pray silently as I walked around the yard, finally sitting down on the stoop in the exhaustion of grief.
>
> Christina got up, saying "church", and walked over to the statue of Our Lady of Grace in front of the house. She patted the statue on the shoulder, then stepped back, crouched down and made the Sign of the Cross alone for the first time. Her little hands clasped tightly, she began to pray. For five minutes, Christina mentioned all of our family members, including my mother as we do in our nighttime prayers. Her little face was a model of concentration as she tightly closed her eyes. It was obvious

that she was praying, not imitating our actions. She has never seen us pray in front of this statue of Our Lady.

When Christina finished her prayers, she made the Sign of the Cross, and again reached out to touch the shoulder of the statue of Our Lady, and when she turned to leave, patted her head affectionately.

I immediately called Mom and Dad to tell them about the prayers of our little saint. They were moved and uplifted by this gesture of love and faith that was so unexpected. Since then, this story has been circulated around my entire family, giving us strength when the darkness threatened to envelop us.

Christina proved that she could pray with words when her mother couldn't. I know God heard us both, but I can't help feeling that the prayers of such innocent children carry a special weight with Jesus who asked the little children to come to Him. Mom was indeed called home last fall, and thanks to the prayers of my little saint, our family realized that as painful as losing her was, she was going home.

As Christina grows in her academic skills and ability to take care of herself, her mother grows in her ability to see with God's eyes, but it doesn't end there. Christina is a gift to be shared with a larger audience; since I shared this story in my column on Catholic Mom.com, has been shared several times on various Catholic radio programs. The simple faith of a child whom the world rejects has served as inspiration for many, who, like her family, are enjoying the gift of Christina. Truly she is a gift from God's Hand.

END NOTES

1. John Allen, Ratzinger's biographer, reports a revelation made by Cardinal Ratzinger at a conference in the Vatican on November 28 1996: "*Ratzinger had a cousin with Down's Syndrome who in 1941 was 14 years old. This cousin was just a few months younger than Ratzinger and was taken away by the Nazi authorities for "therapy" Not long afterwards, the family received word that he was dead,* presumably a victim of "Action T4"one of the 'undesirables' eliminated during that time." [4]

Alicia and Tommy Smith

Chapter 21

An Answer to Prayer

by Alicia Smith

This morning's challenge is that my 9-year-old son, Tommy, and I both wanted to use the computer. I promised him that we would play a reading game later and also go to the library, if he used his time now to read some books while I use a computer. This will be one of the many negotiations that will take place this day to keep the peace and accomplish everything we need and want to do! It is a tough balance, but no different than what goes on in any household that has parents and children—whether they have special needs or not.

I think back to the summer of 1999, when I was at a family reunion in Killington, Vermont. Things could not have been better -- I had a loving husband, my daughter was getting more independent since she had turned five that year, my teaching job was going very well, and it was the middle of summer, a teacher's favorite time of the year. What more could I possibly want? Yet, there seemed to be something missing. Lately, I had begun to have trouble sleeping. I kept waking up at night with a nagging feeling that something was not quite right. I knew that usually meant one thing: that God had a change of plans for me. Whenever something needs to change in my life, this is usually the way He speaks to me I guess it is hard for Him to get my attention!

Maybe it was all the hype about the year 2000 and Y2K, but I was becoming more aware of my increasing age and the passage of time. I thought having my daughter would be enough, but I felt more and more that we should try more seriously for another child. As time went on, I thought about it more and more. My husband was happy with the way things were. After all, he had two older sons from a previous marriage, and now a little girl. He was thinking, "Do we really want to go back to changing diapers and late night feedings and sleep deprivation?"

So, reluctantly, he agreed to try a little more seriously to have another child. After all, more time together is never a bad thing. And lo and behold, by the fall, we were expecting a baby. I felt great and everything seemed to be going just fine. I was teaching school, and the holidays were just around the corner. I was starting to do my Christmas shopping and was very excited about the coming year. Micala, my daughter, was looking forward to helping with a new baby. One evening in the beginning of December 2000, I started to have really painful cramps. I called the doctor right away, and he recommended resting in bed for a few days in hopes that the cramping would subside. It was not to be and I experienced a miscarriage, which was very difficult. I was very sad that this little person whom I had been carrying would not get to experience life outside the womb. I know that she felt our love then and still does to this day.

After a period of time, I was ready to try again. I still felt that this is what God was asking me to do. There was still that missing piece in our lives. So, in April of 2001, I found my husband outside working in the yard. It was a warm and sunny spring afternoon. I told him I had some good news, that I was expecting again. I think he said something like "Already?" I don't think he was quite ready for this again. We were both a little scared after our recent loss last winter.

The pregnancy went smoothly -- I never felt better. I didn't gain too much weight, I was eating healthy foods, getting lots of rest and had no trouble with morning sickness of any kind. I sailed through the first trimester with a sigh of relief. That July, I got invited to swim at a friend's house. The get-together at Janet's home was an annual one, where we would relax and catch up on news, just moms and kids enjoying a summer

94

day. I received so many compliments on how healthy I looked, and I was so enjoying my friends in the sunshine that afternoon. Before long, it was time to make the hour-and-a-half drive back to eastern Connecticut. We said our goodbyes, and then got in the car. I had left my cell phone in the car and I got it out to call Mike, my husband, to tell him that I was on the way home. I noticed that there were several messages from him. I didn't get ahold of him, so I just started back home. His voice sounded serious in the messages, but I didn't think too much about it.

When I returned home, I could see by the expression on his face that something was wrong. Apparently the doctor had called and said that the triple screen blood test had showed some irregular results. He wanted us to think about amniocentesis. The results of the triple screen had indicated that there was a genetic problem with the baby. One of the possibilities was that the baby might have trisomy 21, or Down syndrome. There was also a chance that the baby might have trisomy 13, a serious genetic condition in which the baby would be stillborn, or if it survived the pregnancy, would not live for long.

I prayed and prayed and prayed. It's ironic how your perspective on things can change in an instant and you realize all too well how little control you really have over things in your life. It really lets you know that God is indeed in charge and He has a plan for each and every one of us. I never thought I would ever pray for my baby to be born with Down syndrome, but I had taught children in school with this disability and I felt I could handle that. I'm not sure I could have handled growing attached to my baby for nine months and then having to say good bye right away. That would have been so, so hard.

We decided to have amniocentesis, certainly not to consider terminating the pregnancy, but to have a better idea of what we were facing. I'll never forget my 39th birthday. I was lying in bed, resting after the amniocentesis (what a way to spend your birthday!), but my prayers were answered. The doctors were 99 percent sure that our baby would be born with Down syndrome. It was a bittersweet moment: it seemed that our baby would indeed survive, but what next? I spent the second half of my pregnancy looking up information on-line, and going to the bookstore for anything and everything that I could get my hands on about Down syndrome.

The most shocking thing to me was the obstetrician's attitude. Shortly after we received the results of the amnio, the doctor called. He basically said to me, "Don't worry, Mrs. Smith. We'll make an appointment for you right away and get this taken care of." I was so flabbergasted that I could scarcely reply. I can't believe the doctors assumed that I would want to terminate the pregnancy. I can't remember, but I think I just softly hung up the phone.

The last part of the pregnancy was a busy time. Summer turned to fall, and it was time to go back to school. It was kind of awkward to first tell my colleagues that I was pregnant, and then to tell them about the baby's special needs. But they were so supportive and helped me to get through this trial with resources and love and kindness.

I had been going on the Connecticut Down Syndrome Congress website, which is full of good information about what to expect, and I discovered that their annual conference was to be held in the fall. I registered and attended, feeling a little out of place, but astounded at how I was welcomed. Total strangers came up and hugged me when they found out I was expecting a baby with Down syndrome. They thanked me for moving forward with the pregnancy, and I was thinking to myself, why are they so surprised? It was only later on that I learned about the grim statistic: ninety two percent of babies with Down syndrome are never allowed to be born. It is indeed a tragedy for these babies and the families whose lives would have been changed so positively by their presence.

Tommy's due date was January 11, 2002, but he decided that he did not want to wait that long. All fall and early winter, I had been traveling back and forth to Yale-New Haven Hospital. I was referred to their high-risk clinic due to my age and Tommy's diagnosis. I had been developing an excessive amount of amniotic fluid and even though experts say not to, I looked this symptom up on the internet. I found out that this could be caused by esophageal atresia, which was one of the many medical terms that I would become quite familiar with by the time Tommy was born. This meant that Tommy's stomach was not connected to his esophagus, which also meant that when he was born he would soon need surgery. Many parents of children with Down syndrome are not aware of their children's special needs until the birth, but I considered it a blessing to know so much ahead of time so that my family and I were prepared as much as we could be.

December came and we were getting ready for the holidays. It was a tough time for me because Michael and I were both working, and we had an excited 7-year-old who was looking forward to the Christmas celebration and the new baby with much anticipation. Tommy was born on December 17, 2001. He was whisked away to the NICU, and the next time I saw him, he was lying in a warming tray with tubes and wires, lights flashing and machines beeping. But his piercing eyes looked out at us with happiness, as if to say how glad he was to finally meet us. They seemed to have a quiet strength to them. After a few days, I was released from the hospital. It was the strangest thing to leave the hospital without my baby, for he ended up staying for two months. Michael and Micala and I spent as much time as we could with Tommy.

Since we hadn't expected him to arrive before Christmas, I needed to go out and buy a Christmas stocking for him! We took turns carefully holding him. Michael was better at holding him with all the tubes and wires attached. I could see the love and the bond that was developing between them instantly. And a prouder big sister you will never find. I have a photograph of Micala holding this precious bundle with the sweetest smile on her face. She, too, fell in love with this new addition immediately.

Tommy had as many visitors as the NICU would allow. His Uncle Pete even bought him a new fishing pole, so that some day they could go fishing together. Tommy just recently used his fishing pole for the first time and earned a Cub Scout fishing belt loop. The nurses and staff at the hospital so loved and took such good care of Tommy. He had a feeding tube in his stomach because of his esophageal atresia and many other attachments to help monitor his progress. The NICU was a place of many contrasts. It was a serious place, yet each baby had a little stocking at the end of their crib and Christmas carols played softly in the background. One baby with very serious issues was going home soon. But it was known that the baby was not to survive for long, and the family wanted to spend the baby's last days together. I prayed for that baby and his family and thanked God for my special boy.

Christmas Eve was very hard. We spent as much time visiting with Tommy as we could and then went on to my mom and dad's for the festivities as was our custom. We stayed until about midnight and then it was time to go home. As we passed through New Haven, tears silently streamed down my face; I knew that my baby was there and that we could not be together. But God gave us strength to get through all these tough days.

After surgery and a long stay at the hospital, Tommy was ready to come home in February 2002, the hospital staff was amazing and it was really difficult to say goodbye. They trained us on how to take care of Tommy, so it wouldn't be so scary when we got him home. We threw a lunch party for them, to let them know in some small way, how much they all meant to us.

Fortunately, our medical insurance paid for home nursing care for Tommy so that I could go back to work. It was so hard to go back and trust Tommy to their care, but it worked out well. One of the nurses who cared for him during these early times, Linda, still keeps in touch with us to see how Tommy's doing. When the nursing benefits ran out, we decided that Michael would stay home with Tommy. Financially, this was a difficult time, but we managed through the grace of God to make ends meet, and now the bond they have can never be broken.

If Tommy doesn't feel well, it is still Daddy whom he asks for first. Tommy has changed our lives in so many ways. Michael wanted to make sure that Tommy would have the right services when he became of school age, so he ran for and was elected to the Board of Education, on which he still serves. Micala has been like a junior therapist for Tommy. After the Birth-to-Three therapists came, she would have him do all the activities they did. Even though it took him a long time to reach developmental milestones, I think she helped him reach them a lot sooner. She is thinking of going into the medical field, as she is in the process of choosing a college. Neonatology is a field that really interests her, and I suspect that has a lot to do with Tommy. Micala and I have been more active in the last few years in the pro-life movement. We have gone to Washington, D.C. the last two years for the March for Life, which is a very moving experience.

Now my Tommy is 9 years old and he is quite a character. He is beloved by all who meet him. He can be an affectionate angel who covers you with hugs and kisses and the next minute the most obstinate and grumpy little guy you would ever want to meet. And we would not have it any other way! He has taught us patience and humility that we never thought we would achieve. He was our missing piece and an answer to a prayer, a gift from God that we needed, even though we did not know that's what we needed.

This morning Tommy wakes, as he typically does, in a very cheerful mood. He always says, "Good Morning, Mom! How was your sleep?" He is so happy to greet me, the pets, and the rest of the family each day with enthusiasm. He promptly marches out to the living room, plants himself in front of a basket of toys and announces, "Let's get this party started!" I think to myself, where does he get this from? He's like a little sponge, absorbing everything around him.

From the time he was born, Tommy was very aware of his surroundings. When I look back at pictures of him from his first days in the hospital, I am struck by his alert and beautiful eyes. Despite all the tubes and wires, his expression seemed to say to us, "Don't worry, I am in good hands."

We are proud of the person Tommy is and who he is becoming. He will be in fourth grade in the fall and is a Cub Scout. He made his First Holy Communion last spring. We think he may want to join Special Olympics soon and he really loves bowling. His peers are very patient with him, but sometimes he forgets his manners and does mischievous things, like poking them or getting into their personal space. Although he needs reminders to behave well socially, he is a charming little boy who loves others and just wants love in return. He is truly a gift from God and he has changed our lives forever.

Alicia is an art teacher. She and her husband, Michael, have illustrated a children's book, The Ant with Red Pants.

Lissette and Gracie Yellico

Chapter 22

Our Grace-Filled Miracle

By Lissette Yellico

The ordinary, joyful chaos of our home was in full swing with the anticipation of our fifth baby. Diagnosed with gestational diabetes, I was referred to a high risk specialist. Since this wasn't my first time, I drove to the appointment without any anxiety. I was slightly annoyed that I had to make time for the trip and was looking forward to driving back home as quickly as possible.

After having the ultrasound, the nurse asked me to wait for the doctor to come in. I waited for a long time and started to get nervous. Why was it taking so long for the doctor to come in? I kept telling myself to be calm but I knew in my heart that something was wrong.

The doctor came in and told me the baby had excessive water in her brain and a large hole in her heart. He concluded that the baby had some sort of a chromosomal abnormality, possibly Down syndrome. I felt as if

I was in a daze. "What can I do to help her?" I asked, trying to keep my heart from racing. He told me it was too late. At first I didn't understand what he meant. Then it hit me that he meant an abortion would have taken care of everything. Anger crept in and I answered back, "She's my daughter. God gave her to me." The doctor just stared at me, turned around and began writing a prescription for an amniocentesis. I refused since this carried an increased risk of miscarriage. It was clear to me that the future trips I had to take to this doctor's office would be awkward, since he was clearly upset with my decision to keep my baby.

Holding back tears, I drove home. However, before I got there, peace overtook my soul. I knew that there was a reason why God was blessing us with a special needs child. I thanked Him for the privilege and asked Him for the strength to accept whatever would come to pass.

My husband, Glenn, and I would not give up hope. We felt strong and at peace knowing that we were lifted up by the many prayers from our dear family and friends. My devotion to the Blessed Virgin Mary grew intensely during the last trimester. I felt her prayers for me and motherly care. She wanted me to unite my pregnancy with hers. I began to experience growth in my faith and trust that came from surrendering my will to God's. Although there were brief, dark moments of fear, I couldn't explain to others how much peace I would feel most of the time. My pregnancy became a spiritual retreat.

Glenn and I clung to our prayers as I labored to deliver my baby girl. I heard her loud cry and the hospitals' obstetrician say that she looked alright. Our baby was immediately checked by the neonatologist and she found no immediate problems. The water in her brain had decreased. A few days after her birth, she was checked by a pediatric cardiologist, who was surprised to see that the large hole in her heart had been completely healed. I smiled and thought, "This is a miracle, thanks be to God."

With joy, we named our precious girl Grace Marie, in thanksgiving to the Blessed Mother because I truly felt her presence at my side. She prayed for us and kept us close to her Beloved Son.

Since then, Grace has been diagnosed with epilepsy and ADHD, probably due to the excess water in her brain. However the joy that Gracie's smile brings to our family is without measure. Her brothers and sisters love to take care of her. We are awed by God's wonderful love and mercy. We thank Him for the blessing and joy that a special needs child brings to our family. Our children have learned patience, charity and other virtues needed to bring Christ's love to others. Grace has opened our hearts to so much love.

When I gaze at Grace's beautiful face, I sometimes recall what the doctor had said. If I had listened to him, Grace would not be here. What a terrible emptiness and loss that would have been to our family.

Glenn and Lissette Yellico have been married for 17 years and live with their six gifts from God in North Carolina. The story of Gracie was included in an article entitled, "Moms who never Gave up Hope" in Faith and Family magazine May/June 2007 issue.

Allison and Faith Gringas

Chapter 23

Faith's Story

by Allison Gingras

We had two beautiful sons, but somehow we felt that our family wasn't complete. So we prayed to seek God's will for our family. Our prayers went seemingly unanswered for three years, until an artist shared his own adoption story at a concert one night, and I felt a stirring in my heart. On the way to the car, I told my husband about this overwhelming feeling to open our hearts and home to an orphan. To my delight, he had felt the same tug of the spirit.

After years of prayers and months of paperwork, we could do nothing but wait to hear if a child was available for us to adopt. As a member of the "instant society," a person who taps her foot at the microwave, this would prove to be one of the more difficult aspects of the adoption for me. I tried to settle in for the long haul by likening it to the wait for the births of my sons, but since both pregnancies ended prematurely it wasn't an easy sell. As time passed, and I turned 40, adoption suddenly seemed to be a crazy idea. I spent a lot of time in Eucharistic adoration, questioning my understanding of God's plan. "Did I really hear you correctly Lord, are we REALLY supposed to be adopting at this time in our lives?" The answer in my soul was always a resounding YES!

God was providing us time to prepare for our special child. During a time of prayer, the Holy Spirit told me that our child would be deaf. I had always loved sign language, and as a child had several friends who were deaf. I remember thinking back then that I wanted a deaf child, which seemed such a strange desire. What mother wishes for such a difficulty for her child? Yet the desire was so deeply rooted in my heart that I knew God gave it to me in order to fulfill whatever purpose He held for me and the child He would deliver to me. Continuing to follow the nudges of the Holy Spirit, I enrolled myself in American Sign Language classes.

The Spirit was not done yet. Just days before receiving the referral for my daughter, God softly told me in a dream that the infant I had been praying for, the child that we had adamantly insisted had to be between 9 and 18 months, would be considerably older. I now felt that she would be 3 or 4 years old, and I was heartbroken. I begged God to change His mind, afraid that she'd come with issues I would never be able to handle. Furthermore, I longed to hold an infant again, to feed her a bottle and rock her to sleep; my dreams did not include a preschooler. I woke with such peace, realizing that God's plans are perfect, that an older child did make more sense for our family, which already included a 13- and 10-year-old. I remembered the boys as infants, and how although we loved the infant and the toddler years, they were trying and tiring! If I was honest with myself, I had to admit that we spent much of the time talking about how much fun it would be when they were a little bigger and could do this or that. I actually started to anticipate with joy all these revelations, having decided long ago in this adoption process to trust the Lord with all my heart, mind and soul, and to allow His will to be done.

Two days later, we received a referral for a 3-year-old deaf girl, whom the agency thought might be a good match for our family. I knew instantly that she was my daughter. As her picture materialized on my computer screen, I was even more convinced that she was mine, as she had an uncanny resemblance to my youngest son. Although, the agency encourages people to take at least a 24 hour to make a decision, we requested to be Wu Feng Hua's parents in just five hours!

We had originally been told that we would be traveling to bring our daughter home six to eight weeks following the receipt of our referral. However, unforeseen delays forced us to wait six months before receiving travel approval. I had accepted her being 3 years old, but as time ticked away and she grew closer to 4 years old, my anxiety rose. I also worried that something would happen in the interim and we'd lose her; I had already fallen head-over heels in love!

In July, three months into the wait, I sat on her bedroom floor and prayed the Rosary. As I meditated on the Joyful Mysteries, I heard a strange noise outside the window. As I peered out trying to identify the source, there was the largest butterfly I'd ever seen. Gazing upon this enormous creature, I knew it was a sign from God that all would be well. My eyes filled with tears as I realized that of all the signs God could have sent, the butterfly was perfect—as butterflies are deaf. And if I had any doubts that God was trying to communicate with me, the fruit of the next mystery was, "Faith," the very name we would be giving our daughter! God is such a loving Father. To ensure that I did not lose hope, He sent a butterfly—either a real one, a picture, or the word—every day until the day we met Faith!

The day finally came, October 29, 2009, to board a plane to China, to bring home our new daughter. I still could not believe that God was sending us halfway around the world! The farthest I'd been to this point in my 40 years was Florida, and I hadn't actually enjoyed that two-hour flight! Yet, after a year-and-a-half of waiting to be matched with a child, and six months to get permission to travel, we were on our way. I was filled with great anxiety, but knowing how many people were praying, and the blessings that lay ahead, I had much courage.

A few days after arriving in China, and one of the scariest taxi rides of my life, we found ourselves at the Wuhan Child Welfare Bureau, waiting for the orphanage director to arrive with our daughter. The meeting and hour that passed were surreal, and then much to our amazement, Faith came with us without any tears or protestations.

Wu Feng Hua, now named Faith Feng Hua Gingras, bonded instantly to her new father, but rejected all affection and attempts at contact from me. I was at peace with this for about two days. Then I fell apart, as Faith would just recoil at the mere sight of me.

I remember looking Heavenward saying, "My Lord, why are you doing this to me? Really God, is this really what you sent me half way across the world for? I waited two years to be rejected? All those prayers, all the time and energy, it was for this!"

I was heartbroken, but not hopeless—and so I prayed. I was suddenly struck with the knowledge of what builds trust in relationships. It is the completion of need cycles being met, over and over. I advised my husband that every need she had would be met by me—every morsel of food, drink, potty break, and bath. He'd be her source of affection and comfort, but I would need to be the source of everything else. She may not love me, but she will trust me and eventually see that I am someone upon whom she can depend.

Attachments are also built through skin-on-skin contact, so I took her into the bathtub with me, holding her back against my body in a bear hug, because she would absolutely freak at the sight of me. I would sit, hour after hour, in the tub just praying the Hail Mary repeatedly. Since my daughter was deaf and would not at this time look at me to sign or gesture, I had plenty of opportunity for prayer. I leaned on my Holy Mother for comfort and strength, and she did not let me down!

We finally flew to Guangzhou to meet up with the rest of the adoptive families we'd be traveling with to complete the adoption requirements at the American Consulate. We were blessed to be traveling with another Catholic family, who were happy to join us on Sunday to celebrate the Lord's Day. We each took turns with the Mass readings, and then I suggested we each share an experience during our trip where we had felt God's presence.

I began recounting how earlier that day God had reminded me how, for more than 30 years, despite His attempts to get close to me, I had rejected Him. Yet, He had been patient, and just like I was doing for Faith, had continued to provide my every need-- physically, emotionally and spiritually. I shared that, like God; I would provide unconditional love to my daughter until she was willing to reach out to me. As I finished those words, as though her ears could now hear, she reached her arms out to me for the first time. I let out an audible gasp, and tears flowed from every eye present. The miracle that came from our prayers inspired me to continue to yield to God's will in my life!

Although it wouldn't be until a week after our arrival home that Faith finally accepted me as her new mother, that moment in the Guangzhou hotel was enough to strengthen my faith and resolve to see through whatever lay ahead. One of those joys would be of watching her discover the language that she had been robbed of until this point. Within hours of gaining custody, we had taught her the signs for "kiss," and "potty." Just seven short months later she had a more-than-100-word-sign receptive vocabulary and nearly as large an expressive vocabulary. We have been just amazed at how easily she communicates her basic needs. She is eager to learn sign language and copies new signs and the letters of the alphabet with great determination! We all eagerly await the day when Faith can express her emotions and thoughts, and share whatever memories she may still hold from her life in China.

I think often about her birth mother, the woman who brought my beautiful daughter into this world. How long did it take them to realize she couldn't hear? Whose decision was it to abandon her? Did this mother cry, as she placed her baby down in the parking lot of the hospital, under the cover of night and run away? Did Faith cry in the dark, without the safety of an adult nearby? Are these the thoughts that cause her to wake crying in the middle of the night? She then spent three years in a single foster home. What was her life like there? It's frustrating to receive so little information about her previous life.

Faith is truly a remarkable little girl because after all this, she continues to trust human beings to care for her. She allows us to love her and fully returns that love. It further amazes me that on November 2, 2009, the first time she'd ever laid eyes on us, she let us pick her up, carry her to a cab, and leave with her—all without a single tear. God had to be whispering reassurances into her heart, "These are the parents I have been telling you about, the ones I promised you. Thank you my dear little one for being so patient with My perfect plan."

Allison Gingras is a Catholic wife, homeschool mother of three, writer an inspirational speaker. Allison and her husband, Kevin, have two sons, Ian, 14, and Adam, 11, whom she homeschools, along with Faith. A catechist for over 25 years, Allison recently began writing and speaking on living out our faith in the ordinary, everyday of our lives. In 2009, she launched, Reconciled to You...Finding Our Way Home, a Catholic ministry hoping to inspire people to seek a deeper relationship with God. More about her ministry and presentation topics can be found at www.reconciledtoyou.com , or at Reconciled to You on Facebook.

Gretchen and Simon Peters

Chapter 24

Simon's Story

by Gretchen Peters

"Before I formed you in the womb I knew you; and before you were born I consecrated you." Jeremiah 1:5 (NAB)

Looking back, I can see that God had special motherhood in store for me all along. Isn't it funny how we can go back and see God's work unfolding? I babysat a severely handicapped girl, and did some work with Special Olympics when I was in middle school and during my early years of work. My godmother has a son with Down syndrome. And I always felt as if I was tempting my luck with each pregnancy—there was almost a foreboding. My fourth child even received early intervention services for a short period of time due to a delay in rolling over.

God had led me onto the path before I realized what was happening. I knew that He was asking me to walk this road, but that didn't make it any easier. At least not right away. My name is Gretchen and my husband, Jim, and I have five children. Our youngest, Simon, was born in December

2004 with Pallister-Killian syndrome, a rare chromosomal disorder caused by the presence of four copies of the short arm of chromosome 12, instead of the usual two. The disorder affects children in a multitude of ways, including mental retardation, developmental delays, hearing loss, a flattened nasal bridge, a high forehead, and many other traits. In Simon's case, it has left him vision and hearing impaired, globally delayed, and mentally handicapped. He also has seizures and low muscle tone, which makes it difficult for him to control his body. At 7 years old, he cannot sit, crawl, chew or communicate. What he can do is use *his* special abilities to make us smile. We love to hear his laugh and we receive great hope from his simple joy.

Simon has one brother, Alex, who is nearly 2, and three sisters: Emily,19, Maddy, 13, and Natalie, 8. There were ups and downs early on about having a sibling with special needs, but they now understand that he's still their brother and as deserving of love, care and opportunities as every other child God creates. In fact, they love to show him off, bring him to school and teach others about PKS.

Simon was diagnosed in utero at about five months. During a routine sonogram, doctors noticed that he had short bones, a cleft lip and enlarged brain ventricles. Amniocentesis was negative for trisomies 13, 18 and 21, but a closer look revealed a problem with chromosome 12. Doctors shipped Simon's cells to the Mayo Clinic, where a diagnosis of PKS was made. The news knocked me flat. I prayed as I had never prayed before. Each morning, I woke depressed and hopeless until I sat down and looked over Bible verses and spiritual readings. Every time I felt myself falling, I prayed. Honestly, I felt better almost as soon as I began. I added our baby to the prayer list at church, and many others did the same for us. Knowing that prayers for Simon and our family were heading to Heaven soothed me. I remember how I struggled to say, "Let me do your will, God." I remember thinking that if I said it that meant it was real! It would be true, and I didn't want it to be true.

Gradually, however, the prayer, "Not my will, Lord, but Thine," became part of my daily and hourly petitions. Once I said it, it was as though a burden lifted off my shoulders. I knew that God held us in His hands and would carry us through the challenges that lay ahead. During the pregnancy, Jim was my other source of strength. He kept me from imagining the worst and was sure to think of ways our future would be bright.

After Simon was born, when I "hit the ground running" to get Simon the medical and therapeutic services he needed, Jim needed time to deal with his own feelings. He had been so caring of me that he needed to process this new life for himself. He's a great dad, who is very involved in the care of Simon and all our children, and continues to be an amazing husband.

God continues to take care of us. Every doubt I have is answered by Him. A Bible verse speaks to me at the right time; a Gospel reading reminds me that God is there. A friend arrives at just the right time.

One day, shortly after Simon was born, Father Naas, our parish priest, came over for coffee. I was talking about my sadness and he said, "Well, we don't know that Simon *wanted* to walk, drive, hold a job, or go to Europe, do we?" What he was saying is that the loss isn't Simon's; the loss is ours—our perception of what life *should* be. There is no need to feel sorry for Simon. He doesn't know that he's missing out on anything! He loves his little world and is very happy. Father also told me to live in the moment. How true! Don't worry about 10 or 20 years from now. Who knows if we will even be here? Love Simon now and worry about tomorrow, tomorrow.

> "Do not worry about tomorrow; tomorrow will take care of itself."
> Matthew 6:34 NABRE

See, God has laid it all out for us. And I know I'm not alone. Jesus walks with me, as does His mother, Mary.

Singer Amy Grant's song *Breath of Heaven* has been a favorite of mine for many years, but it truly spoke to my heart on the day I was discharged from the hospital after giving birth to Simon. We were on the way to see him in the neonatal intensive care unit at a hospital in a nearby town. It was near Christmas, so we had our Christmas CDs playing in the car. That song started, and tears just poured from my eyes. The song describes the thoughts Mary carried along with her on that fateful journey to Bethlehem.

Mary knew! Mary wondered about the great task God had chosen her for! What if she had said no? The minute I heard that song was the minute I moved forward. I mourned, but realized that I wasn't the first to give birth to a child with special needs. Many suffer much greater hardships than I or Simon. I, too, had those questions, those fears. But if Mary could place her faith in our Father, how could I do any less?

Simon's challenges have been great, but he is doing relatively well. When he was born, he spent a little time in an oxygen tent because he was having trouble maintaining his oxygen levels. He also had a slight heart murmur. Within a few days, both problems had disappeared. He had a few episodes of apnea, in which he stopped breathing for one to two minutes, but that also rectified itself. Six days after he was born, we took Simon home. And two months later, he had surgery to repair his cleft lip. We learned to be grateful for these small victories. Simon started school when was 2 years and 8 months old. For five years, he has been working hard in a great school that he attends every day. He receives occupational, physical, hearing, vision and speech therapy at school. When he's home, he's allowed to be himself. Simon loves to swim and for a short time took horse-back riding lessons to help his balance and core strength. He enjoys listening to music and swinging. We've seen some nice progress lately. In December 2009, he learned to drink from a straw and in early 2010 we saw marked improvement in weight bearing—so much so that school is slowly introducing a gait trainer.

I know Simon has a long way to go, but God has blessed us with progress! The greatest challenge about being Simon's parents is his total dependence on us for his care. We do not qualify for any assistance for financial help or care giving. Right now, Simon is still small enough that carrying him is not too difficult, but he will eventually grow too large. He needs to be dressed, diapered, bathed, etc. He is unable to lift himself, sit or stand. Our house is in no way handicapped accessible. We'll need a handicapped van soon. The monetary ramifications are staggering. I'm praying that with God's help we'll find a way to get what we need when the time comes.

The day I found out about Simon is truly the day when I cemented my Catholic faith. I've grown in grace, faith and love for God. I knew I was filled with God's graces the day that I realized I would not choose to exchange Simon's PKS for a "normal" child. If I were to do that it would be for me, not for him. Oh, there are some moments and some days when I'd give anything for Simon to look at me, realize I'm his mom and smile at me. But in the end, I know what's more important. Simon has already attained what the rest of us strive for every day. He's already a saint, a pure and holy soul bound for Heaven.

Looking back (isn't hindsight wonderful?) I again see a little of God's work in our lives. After about 14 years of marriage, my husband converted to the Catholic faith. Just a few years later, Simon was born. I think God knew that Jim would need a greater faith life to handle the trials coming our way. Our entire family is firmly rooted in our Church. My 22-year-old son became an altar server, and 19-year-old Emily attends retreats through our youth group. Is any of this because of Simon? I don't know, but it's a beautiful thing!

Should Simon die before I do, well, I know that I'll have a saint in Heaven praying for me. And *then* he'll smile at me and call me "Mom".

Gretchen Peters is a cradle Catholic who is <u>still</u> learning about her faith. She works part-time at a college library and full-time as a non-paid director of PKS Kids, a non-profit organization she and several other parents started to raise awareness of Pallister-Killian Syndrome. She is happily married with five kids and lives in Michigan.

Kim and Abby Garvin

Chapter 25

Answering the Call

by Kim Garvin

Life is like a puzzle—and God is slowly handing me the pieces. That's how it was during my childhood search for belonging, and when, as a young adult, I finally began attending Mass regularly. And that is how I feel today as the mother of three young children, one of whom has Down syndrome and related medical problems. I look at Abbey's challenges as pieces of the puzzle that God is revealing to me, little by little.

He began laying out the design of this puzzle when I was just a child. While I am a lifelong Catholic, my family did not attend Mass regularly. My mom is Catholic, but my dad did not practice any formal religion. He did, however, support my mom. So, my siblings and I were baptized in the Church and received all the sacraments. But I needed more.

I remember wanting so strongly to belong to something that I even went to youth group meetings at a friend's non-Catholic church. Then I went to college and stopped attending church completely. But when I returned home after graduation, I started attending Mass again and even volunteered as a religious education teacher. I remember always feeling a call to be closer to God and to grow in my faith. I just didn't know how to go about it.

In 1999, when I was 29 years old, I moved from New Jersey to Kentucky and joined Blessed Mother Catholic Church in Owensboro. There was an active youth group there, which turned out to be just what I needed. Not only did I grow in the Faith, but I met my husband through this group. God had finally begun revealing His plans for me. I attended daily Mass, stayed active as an adult volunteer with the youth group, taught religious education classes, helped out with RCIA and more. This time strengthened my faith in God and the Church. What I didn't know at the time was that God was preparing me for the greatest challenge of my life: becoming a special mother.

Steve and I were married in October 2002 and decided to live in Owensboro. Not long after the honeymoon, we discovered that we were expecting our first child. Things proceed normally until our 20- week prenatal ultrasound. That's when the technician spotted something unusual about the baby's heart and we were referred to a high-risk obstetrician in Louisville, KY.

We were very anxious as we traveled two hours to Louisville to meet with the doctor. I remember thinking that this isn't how we were supposed to spend our first pregnancy. The doctor did an ultrasound and confirmed an abnormality known as atrioventricular canal defect, or AV canal for short. This is basically a large hole in the center of the heart, along with a single valve—instead of the usual two—between the upper and lower chambers. This causes oxygen-rich blood to mix with blood that carries no oxygen. The heart has to work extra hard to bring oxygen to the body, thus causing an enlarged heart and other symptoms. The doctor explained that AV canal is often associated with Down syndrome, but not always. She added that she didn't see any other signs of Down syndrome from the ultrasound.

At some point in this process, the high-risk obstetrician said that the only way to be sure that our baby had Down syndrome was to do an amniocentesis. She explained that amniocentesis performed before 32 weeks poses the risk of miscarriage. After 32 weeks, the risk shifts to preterm birth which, while still risky, gives the baby a better chance of survival. We decided to wait until the 32-week mark.

The results took a few weeks, but we were already preparing ourselves for the news. I remember the day we found out for sure. I was at a regularly scheduled check-up in Owensboro when the obstetrician in Louisville called. My doctor took the call and shared that the baby had Down syndrome and was a girl. I remember being sad, but not surprised. We had resigned ourselves to this outcome. I got in the car and called my husband to tell him the news. We met at home and cried together.

We spent the next month learning about Down syndrome and connecting with the local support group, which was awesome! I am so thankful that we knew about Abbey having Down syndrome and her heart condition before her birth. We were able to prepare ourselves and our families. This was the time I felt both close to God and far from God. My faith was tested over and over as I questioned, "Why me? Why us?" but then someone would remind me that God doesn't give us things we can't handle. During these last few weeks we grieved and prepared and tried to muster up excitement about the birth of our daughter.

Since we knew Abbey had a heart defect, we planned an induced delivery in Louisville, two hours from our home, where there was a children's hospital and pediatric specialists immediately available. Abigail Elizabeth was born on July 3, 2003. She weighed 5lbs 6oz and if you didn't know she had a heart defect, you wouldn't have known. Everything seemed pretty "normal" at first. She was doing well and feeding by bottle for almost a week before she encountered feeding issues, so the doctor inserted a feeding tube.

She remained in Kosair Children's Hospital neonatal unit for six weeks. During this entire time we lived at the Ronald McDonald House and walked back and forth to the hospital for feedings. We spent as much time as we could at the hospital, but there is only so much you can do in a neonatal unit. We learned how to do some of the normal first baby things like changing diapers, giving baths, etc. except we had to do it while being careful of a feeding tube and heart monitor wires. While this time was difficult, it also brought me some special graces. A neonatal unit is a place that, until my daughter was there, I never really knew existed. There were so many babies fighting for their tiny lives. Some didn't even have people there to visit them. It really put things in perspective for me. Abbey wasn't fighting for her life. We knew her stay there was going to be brief not months long like some babies. I still have a place in my heart and in my prayers for neonatal babies and their families.

Abbey's ups and downs with feeding and weight gain were the primary reasons she stayed at the hospital for so long. We finally took her home at six weeks of age with a feeding tube, special formula, and lots of medicine for her heart. Bringing Abbey home was both exciting and terrifying. We had family and friends around to help, and home health professionals to teach us how to feed her and attend to her medical needs. To make a difficult situation worse, we needed to be very careful of germs. This was hard on us because we, too, were "quarantined" to some extent. I remember being sad at times because we couldn't do all of the typical fun things you might do with your new baby.

We often thank God that He sent us Abbey first. The care she needed with feedings, therapies and doctor visits was overwhelming at times. This was so much work that I couldn't really enjoy my baby. It was nice to be home, but times were tough.

We were in and out of the hospital for feeding and infection issues, but the most significant issue occurred when Abbey developed congestive heart failure. Fluid collected around her heart, making it difficult for the organ to pump efficiently. We knew this would happen at some point, and it was pretty scary to be living two hours from her doctors. They had explained the signs of congestive heart failure to us, and we noticed them at home in late September 2003. The cardiologists felt it was too early for Abbey to have open heart surgery, so they decided to give her a pulmonary artery band, which helped to restrict the amount of blood flowing through the artery. This was not open-heart surgery, but it was serious. The surgeon had to open Abbey's rib cage and hook her up to breathing tubes. This was the worst thing I had ever experienced. Seeing her hooked up to all those machines was heartbreaking.

We spent another six weeks in the hospital, again in intensive care, because her lungs kept filling up with fluid. The cardiologist had to do three bronchoscopes to clear her lungs before we could finally take her home.

This, too, was an experience I will never forget. The children in intensive care and their families all had their own stories and challenges. The death of a little girl who shared the room with Abbey gave me a glimpse into how blessed we actually were.

The next year was filled with many doctor visits to Louisville and therapy services at home. Both Steve and I worked at this time so his mother took care of Abbey for us. Thank goodness for the respite nurse who gave Grandma a break during the week. There were so many things we learned in the first year—things I never expected to encounter. It became so overwhelming, that we decided that the best thing to do was for Steve to quit his job and stay home with Abbey so that one of us could keep track of all of her appointments. Still, today, this has been a huge benefit for everyone. But, the fact that I am the sole breadwinner for our family can be stressful for me. It is in these times of stress that I get reminded that this is God's plan, not mine.

In January 2005, when I was six months pregnant with our second child, doctors repaired Abbey's AV canal. The surgery was a resounding success, and she stayed in the hospital for just eight days this time. To us, this was amazing. All of our other hospital experiences were so long and difficult. This time, she was bigger and stronger, and healed like a champ.

Eight years later, Abbey's heart is still doing well. We need to visit the cardiologist just once a year now. Although we have had a few rough winters with respiratory syncytial virus (RSV) and pneumonia, resulting in a few hospitalizations, her health has taken a turn for the better since 2007. The biggest hurdle we face now is the fact that Abbey is hearing impaired. She has some hearing capability with hearing aids but is delayed in speech and language. This challenge presents us with extra therapy and behavioral issues.

Today, our family includes 5-year-old Alex and 3-year-old Andrew. Abbey is doing well at seven. Aside from the fact that she doesn't use many words to communicate she makes us laugh a lot and she finds ways to get her needs met. She has a smile and a little giggle that just makes my heart melt. It is in those quiet moments when she is connecting with me in wordless ways that I feel so blessed. She loves her brothers and is a big help around the house. Abbey loves to play outside, look at books, draw and watch TV. She is also very mischievous and gets into her fair share of trouble.

Through everything, my faith has been a great source of strength. I can't tell you how many people said to me, especially during the first year of Abbey's life, "I don't know how you do it!" After finding out my baby was not going to be the way I expected her to be, I just put my faith in God: I knew that He had a reason for bringing this little girl into our lives. God's grace has helped me to accept the challenges that having a child with Down syndrome brings.

Being a Catholic provides me with plenty of opportunity to strengthen that faith. Going to Mass, celebrating the life, death and resurrection of Jesus and receiving the Eucharist brings me such joy and grace which help me to face whatever might come my way. I was going to daily Mass at the time I was pregnant with Abbey, and I know that continuing to stay connected to the Eucharist was the reason I survived the tough times. Another source of my strength was our parish community. There was an outpouring of love and prayers for us and for Abbey during those first difficult years.

There are two beautiful saints that I look to for guidance and strength as a woman and a mother; Mary, the Blessed Mother and Saint Gianna Beretta Molla. I ask Mary to pray for me to live out God's plan the way He wants me to and to love the way I am supposed to love. Saint Gianna Beretta Molla was an amazing wife, mother and physician who gave life in caring for others and ultimately gave her life to save her unborn baby. She is the ultimate role model of the working mom and a true witness to the sanctity of life.

Along this journey, I have learned many things. My faith is stronger than I thought. I can honestly say that if this story had been described to me ten years ago, I would have said that I couldn't handle it. Prayer and the Eucharist can sustain us through anything. I have confidence that God will continue to call me closer to Him in His own way, through my vocation as a special mother.

Kim Garvin is a married, working mother of three living in Knoxville, TN, where they attend All Saints Catholic Church. Kim can be contacted at khgarvin@gmail.com

Diane and Mary Ellen Grover

Chapter 26

Welcome to Rome

by Diane Grover

If you speak to a parent who has a child with Down syndrome, they will likely be able to tell you how they felt when they first read the poem *Welcome to Holland*, by Emily Kingsley. Written by the mother of a young man who has Down syndrome, the poem tells us that we are on a journey. Kingsley writes that although we expected to land in Italy, we have actually arrived in Holland. We learn that both destinations are equally beautiful, just drastically different from each other. It is a wonderful lesson about expectations and acceptance.

When I heard this poem for the first time, I was moved. Its message comforted me in the knowledge that although we had not landed where we expected, we would be fine in our new home. And as time went by, this poem began to take on new meaning for my husband and me. We realized that we had, indeed, landed in Italy after all. Rome, Italy. As we reminisce about our experience, we agree that it is not the tulips of Holland we are looking at, but the basilicas of Rome.

The eternal city is even more beautiful than we expected. It is almost as if God announces over the plane's loudspeaker, "Welcome to Rome. I will be your traveling companion. You have nothing to fear." My husband and I grabbed our guidebooks-the Church's teachings-and held them tightly. With our daughter Mary Ellen as our tour guide, we see the breathtaking hills and valleys of our new location. We take in the richness of Rome's churches, shrines, museums and ruins. Each day we learn more than the day before. Yes, we have landed in Rome; how sweet it is!

Our lessons came quickly in our new destination. As pilgrims, we would learn more than ever before. In our first lesson, we learned about God's unconditional love. Following the birth of our daughter, one of the nurses shared with us how frequently children with Down syndrome are aborted. She was telling us how beautiful our daughter is and simply blurted this out. In that moment, I realized that not everyone would value my daughter or love her as deeply as we already did.

While staring at our newest treasure from God, I could not help but think of my own imperfections, which I know are part of me. I thought deeply about the love that God has for me, imperfections and all. The words of John whirled through my head. "Just as the Father has loved Me, I have also loved you; abide in My love," (John 1:9 NASB) It was so easy to love our precious daughter. She is a gift from God. God had unconditionally loved us all these years. Our youngest daughter helped us to understand the depth of His love for us. We know that although all of us are imperfect, He loves us. We understand this love more now than we ever had before.

Our second lesson in Rome came rather quickly after the first. Although we love our child unconditionally, we knew that some things are outside of our control. Questions rolled through our minds. Will our daughter walk? Will she talk? Will she know God? It was in these moments that we realized we must surrender it all to God; we must humbly hand it all over to Him. He created this child for His purpose. He created this child for His plans. Whatever comes will happen in His time and in His way.

In this lesson we learned to surrender, and we were schooled in humility. "The poor and humble surrender to the loving will of the Father, in ever deeper union with His beloved Son," as the *Catechism of the Catholic Church* states in paragraph 2712. When we were able to do this, we were able to love more fully, more unconditionally. That first lesson blossomed more completely in the second lesson. We opened ourselves to God's will. In doing so, we found the peace we needed to wholly accept our daughter, exactly as God had created her. We were able to take pleasure in all of her little baby stages. We are so grateful for this surrender because, as she grew, we realized that she is more like our other children than she is unlike them. It would have been a waste to spend this time worrying, instead of enjoying our little baby.

Our journey to Rome did not end there. At four-and-a-half months of age, our tour guide went into heart failure. Our third lesson had begun, and we were instructed very clearly on our prayer life. When we brought our little darling to the pediatric cardiologist, we learned that she had a little hole in her heart. Well, it is amazing what a little hole can do to a little heart! At this point, she would teach us all how to handle heart failure and how to patiently wait until she was six months old for open-heart surgery. Our prayer life increased in every way during this time. We learned that St. John Chrysostom was right when he said, "It is possible to offer fervent prayer even while walking in public or strolling alone, or seated in your shop, while buying or selling, or even while cooking." While we waited for our turn to have this open-heart procedure, prayer was as present as breathing.

Our family has always been a prayerful family. However, during this time, every thought was offered up as a prayer. Truly, this prayer carried us through the waiting period. We implored the saints to pray for us as well. In moments when we were unable to pray, we sent out emails asking friends and family to pray. Many Masses were celebrated for us during this time. The power of these prayers carried us. St. John Chrysostom was right again when he said, "Nothing is equal to prayer; for what is impossible it makes possible, what is difficult is easy." While I would not say waiting was easy, I will say that it was possible. It was much more endurable because of the prayers.

All of these lessons came to us when we took a surprise detour to Rome. The "Vatican" is truly as tremendous as everyone says it is. Our Holy Father is doing a wonderful job shepherding his flock and upholding Church teaching on the dignity of all life. The artwork in Rome is absolutely stunning. Paintings and murals depicting the infant Jesus will never look the same again. If you look at them very closely, you might actually think that you are seeing the beautiful almond-shaped eyes of an individual with Down syndrome. Perhaps the artists were wise enough to use such a person as their model.

Our family is ever grateful to have learned many lessons about Rome in the years following our darling Mary Ellen's birth. Landing in this place has brought those lessons to life. We will forever be grateful for our trip to Rome. And we are eternally thankful for the adorable little tour guide that God sent us. Indeed, we are blessed.

Diane Grover is the founder of International Down syndrome Coalition for Life. She tells her story in the "Special Mothers Respond" chapter of this book. She lives with her family in South Carolina.

Kimberlee and Eliza Kadar-Kallen

Chapter 27

Happy Birthday Eliza!

by Kimberlee Kadar-Kallen

As I write this, our Eliza sweetie pie is 4 years old today! As with any child's birthday, it's amazing to think of how the years have flown by and yet it's also hard to remember what life was like before having her.

But I do remember. I remember well the dreadful pain and sorrow that so many of us know far too well of losing a little one to miscarriage. And the deep dark place I was left in as we waited and longed so for a new little one to join us on this earth. I remember pleading with St. Faustina as I was blessed with her relic on Divine Mercy Sunday. And I remember the exceedingly great joy when after a year-and-a-half of waiting we were finally found to be with child. I remember the phone call in which my doctor told us our little one had a heart defect and likely had trisomy 21 as well. I remember hanging up the phone and saying to Michael, "Honey, we're goin' to Holland!" And we waited with wonder that we had been chosen for this special task and curiosity to see what this baby with a little 'something extra' would be like.

We had six ultrasounds in all but we never peeked to see if we'd be having a boy or a girl. I so wanted a girl as I knew this special one would need lots of extra care and attention and would be closest in age to three big sisters. But my doctor had once referred to baby as 'he', and though she denied it, I thought she knew something I didn't. As my due date approached we decided to induce via amniotomy as we really wanted this baby to be born in the hospital, in case special care was needed. I went in at seven in the morning and my doctor thought for sure I'd have a baby by noon.

Not so. I was doing marathon speed walking up and down the hospital corridors for hours, pausing and pleading every time I passed the statue and relic of St. Gerard in the hallway. At around 2:30 p.m., as the Hour of Mercy approached, it began to gradually dawn on me in my foggy-brained state that perhaps there was some chance we were going to have a girl. Our little Elizabeth Faustina arrived at 3:44 p.m.! She didn't make a peep but she was pink as could be. We were all overjoyed to have her here!

I had made this tiny white hat for the new baby, with a blue pompom tied on the top and a pink bow on the front. We whipped that blue pom pom right off and put the little hat on our little pink princess!

That evening, our wonderful pastor kindly came out to the hospital to baptize her. I always say that's one baptism I remember what the baby's mother wore (and no, you can't see a picture of me in my blue bathrobe). Other than briefly turning blue and scaring her mother and nurse, she did quite well that first night. We took her to the nursery so the nurse could keep an eye on her. I remember sitting in the rocking chair with my little silent baby, watching the nurses change and feed and try to soothe the other newborns as they bleated and wailed and shrieked their displeasure at the cruelties of life outside the womb. My little one had no energy with which to cry. Or nurse. I would work so hard to get her to latch on, only to have my triumph dissolve as she fell back to sleep after a minute or so. One nurse remarked about my determination as I held Eliza's little chin for guidance, "She'll get it," she encouraged. She sure did.

Miss Eliza, Queen of Cuteness, has certainly come a long way since her first night in my arms. She certainly has plenty of energy now. She is such a special blessing in so very many ways. She makes people happy every day just by flashing her infectiously joyous grin and adding a squeeze of a hug for good measure. She keeps us lighthearted. She makes us laugh. She makes us pray. She so clearly makes known the wisdom and love and generosity and goodness of her Creator. She makes us so very thankful for this very special gift which she is.

Kimberlee Kadar-Kallen lives in Pennsylvania with her husband and seven children, whom she has always homeschooled. The story about Eliza was originally posted on her blog a www.ponderedinmyheart.typead.com, where she writes about life with her music-, nature-, art-, book- and Eliza-loving family. Her lighthearted article about Eliza, 'Special Blessings, Special Vocabulary', can be found at www.benotafraid.net.

Helen and Colette Dilworth

Chapter 28

The Triumph of the Cross

by Helen Dilworth

Those familiar with the adoption process won't be surprised to hear that one of our six adopted children suffers from Reactive Attachment Disorder. A psychologist painted a vivid, mental image of this condition when he described my child as living in a wheelchair that no one else can see. It is hard for those who have not lived with a RAD child to truly fathom the relentless and unforgiving aspects of this condition. In spite of the daily challenges which this condition presents, I have continued to long for more children - and lots of them! I wasn't sure if this desire was part of my own disordered fervor or an inspiration from the Lord.

Consequently, my prayerful cry was, "Is it right, Lord, to adopt more children if You have already challenged my patience, my virtue, my love with such a demanding child? Is it right to bring more children into our family when one requires heroic forbearance by his young siblings?" I reflected that natural fertility is not removed from a couple if one child is born with special needs. I concluded that having one child with special needs is not a reason, in itself, to stop having children.

"Marriage is an unbreakable bond for the expression of fidelity and the raising of Christian children." I remembered these words of St. Augustine describing the vocation I had been given. Marriage, by its very essence, includes children. I found more support in continuing to have children in the *Catechism of the Catholic Church*, "In this sense the fundamental task of marriage and family is to be at the service of life." CCC#164.

While this question pestered me for an answer, and the insistent desire for more children continued its assault, I attended one of my formation meetings with the Franciscans of the Immaculate. We were taught that married couples should always pray for children. This prayer is a way for married couples to practice chastity within marriage.

To me, it seemed much easier to discern "open to life" when one has the natural gifts required to have children. I had long ago considered myself barren-as-a-stone. What was I to do? I didn't have this gift of fertility (or so I thought). I could add the prayer to my life, even if it seemed incompatible to me to pray to have children biologically.

I decided that practicing openness to life meant maintaining current paperwork in the adoption process, doing my best to follow up on adoption leads, and investigating the recommendations of friends regarding agencies. I have believed that doing my best to offer a "yes" to God allowed the Master greater reign in my life. My "yes" allows God to say "yes" or "no." My "yes" means I am open–available for more.

With my husband's willingness and consent, we continued to apply to adoption programs. We did not ask explicitly for special-needs children, but we were fully aware that children who come from orphanages or foster care may very well arrive in wheelchairs that cannot be seen.

An interesting twist to this story developed last year with my surprise pregnancy. My doctor told me that I was a carrier for cystic fibrosis. This was surprising news. I was unaware of any family members who had CF. We knew, however, that my husband was a carrier for this genetic condition, so this gave us a one-in-four chance that our baby would be a special-needs child.

I didn't think in pregnancy that my child would have CF. I concentrated on the 75 percent chance that the child would be born free of this condition, a condition which affects the lungs and digestive system. The Lord had given us a houseful of children to care for, I reasoned, and the newest had entered our family just a few months earlier. I was also dreadfully sick the entire pregnancy. How could I possibly be strong enough to care for a medically fragile child? How could this be God's will for us?

But the Lord's ways are not my ways. I was not thinking with the mind of God. He did bless our family with a medically fragile child. In some ways, I feel that the Lord answered the prayerful question I have asked throughout my marriage. "Should I continue to have children despite special needs?" He answered loudly and in the affirmative.

The Lord loves special-needs children. He loves families who are open to life no matter what the cost. He loves hearts which open further when pried by special needs. He gives abundant graces to those who carry their crosses. He brings them more and more into Himself.

The Lord loves special needs, and we should not be afraid to embrace life for fear of special needs. Openness to life despite special needs is a true reflection of The Triumph of the Cross.

Helen Dilworth and her family live in Connecticut. She writes a blog called "Castle of the Immaculate" and a daily Marian meditation which she calls "Mary Vitamin".

Gianna and Nicola Moore

Chapter 29

Gianna's Story

by Nicola Moore

Pregnant with my third child, I was feeling a little overwhelmed yet excited. My first child would be under 3 when my third was born. I prayed that I would be able to cope. I had experienced some sharp pain in my side early in the pregnancy, and so the doctor asked for my gall bladder to be checked at the same time as my standard 20-week ultrasound. The sonographer appeared very agitated during the scan and walked out at one stage. Just after she returned, a doctor entered and told the sonographer to "get a grip." I was a bit disturbed by the lack of professionalism, but concluded that the young woman must have been having personal problems, and left the ultrasound unconcerned.

The next day, my family doctor called, saying that he needed to discuss the results with me as soon as possible. I worried about how gall stones would be treated during pregnancy. The doctor gently told me that there were no signs of gall stones, but that the ultrasound of the baby showed "lemon shaping of the head consistent with neural crest defects." Holding back tears, I asked what this would mean for the baby. "Hydrocephalus, spina bifida or anencephaly are all possibilities," the doctor replied. "Do you want to continue the pregnancy?" Shocked that he would even suggest this only minutes after telling me the bad news, I told him bluntly that I don't kill my kids and never to bring it up again. I gathered my thoughts quickly and asked if we could at least do further testing and get more information. He booked me for a high-level ultrasound at a major hospital.

The five days we spent waiting for that ultrasound were torture. I cried out to God from the depths of my heart. I couldn't believe that after years of faithfulness to Him that He would repay me with a severely disabled child. "Surely, God, I deserve better than this," I cried. I was distraught at the prospect of having three children under 3, including one with severe disabilities. Those were dark days; I was so angry at God. As has always been the case when I am burdened, I turned to my mother for support. She was and is the wisest person I have ever met. I poured out my heart to her, looking for sympathy. Instead, she spoke words that cut me down to size! "What right do we have," she said, "to assume that God should only give children with disabilities to other people?" Mum's words stabbed right through my self-righteousness, and the truth of her wisdom had an immediate impact. I knew she was right. It was like a cloud lifted from my heart and head and the anger at God melted away. Although I remained anxious at what lay ahead, I knew that the sentiments of Job are true. If we take blessings from the hand of the Lord, should we not take sorrow also?

We drove four hours to the high-level ultrasound, but with some peace in our hearts. As the technician began checking the baby's brain, a professor of fetal medicine entered the room. He picked up the original ultrasounds and grimly shook his head. His words stunned me. "There is nothing wrong with this baby; the original ultrasounds are just badly done!" They continued to carefully examine the child within me, and assured me that he was just fine! I went home relieved and happy, but changed, and Kiernan James arrived, the easiest and most perfect little bundle imaginable!

The following years brought two more boys, and my hands were full. We moved house several times, and had just arrived in a new town, far from all family and friends, when I found out I was pregnant again. I was exhausted from moving and from caring for five children under the age of 8. As if this wasn't enough, Aidan, not quite 3, had attention deficit disorder and was as much work as all the other children put together! Although I loved being a mother, and Jeff and I had always wanted a large family, we both felt that at the end of each day we had nothing left to give to another child. At this time, we had just purchased land and were making plans to build a house. We felt stretched to our limits. I seriously questioned God's wisdom in giving us another baby. "I can barely cope with what we have, I complained, let alone be good parents to another child." I cried for weeks when I was on my own, feeling abandoned by God.

As the pregnancy progressed and I felt tired and achy, I did what I could to feel positive about having another child. At 28 weeks I had an ultrasound to check the height of the placenta. I had enough experience with ultrasounds by then to know that something was not right. The technician seemed to be taking much longer than normal, and she kept leaving the room and returning to take more pictures. I asked if there was a problem and she said everything was fine; she just needed more pictures of the placenta. But I knew she was not looking at the placenta. The usual black circle of the baby's stomach appeared on the screen, with another circle that looked much the same beside it. I knew I had not seen this on previous ultrasounds. When she was finally done, I walked out in the waiting room to find a friend there. Bursting into tears, I blurted out, "There is something wrong with the baby's stomach."

An appointment with the doctor the next day confirmed my fears—the baby had duodenal atresia, with the duodenum not attached to the intestines and thus distended, looking like a second stomach on the ultrasound. "Can't they just fix that?" I asked. "Yes, certainly, but there's more," the doctor continued. "One in three babies with this condition also has Down syndrome." I felt like I had been knocked down by a truck. I drove home in tears and called Jeff. I knew for sure now that God had taken leave of His senses because coping with a sixth child was one thing; coping with a child with extra needs was way beyond what I had the energy for at that point. I cried and wallowed in self pity. Once again, I was angry at God. How on earth could I cope?

I thought back to the experience a few years before, and the words of wisdom Mum had shared. Almost instantly a peace came upon me. Somehow, in the depth of my heart, I knew that my child would have Down syndrome, and that somehow everything would be okay. Almost instantly I stopped crying and never cried again.

In the following months, I reflected on how God had worked in my life, and it seemed that so much had been arranged to prepare me for what lay ahead. I had obtained a degree in special education, and even at the time I had an uneasy feeling that I would use this for my own purposes. I also completed a sub-major in speech and language disorders, and had spent a year studying physiotherapy. I had worked for many years with children and adults with disabilities, many with Down syndrome. It seemed that somehow all of that was just God's preparation for this next step in my life. Though there was still a lot of anxiety about how I would cope, a certain peace descended on our home. Throughout this time, Jeff just believed that everything was going to be fine. In his mind, I'm sure this meant the baby being born without Down syndrome!

Within days of learning that my baby had problems, I mentioned the situation to a play group coordinator. He contacted the coordinator of a service that links volunteers to young mothers in need of support. Shortly thereafter, she turned up on our doorstep to see how she could help me. She concluded that I needed more than a volunteer. The next day, I received a visit from someone who ran a service that provides government funded childcare in people's homes. A woman named Jo, with whom I immediately felt comfortable, began working in our house and getting to know the children. Jo brought a joy and calm to our house and became like an older sister to me. Jo has recently moved on to working with another family, after working in our home morning and evening for more than seven years. She was most certainly part of God's plan for us. It is clear that God did know what He was doing in giving me another child!

As the weeks rolled by, my baby was unable to swallow any amniotic fluid. My belly began to swell as the fluid built up inside, and the doctor warned that a premature birth was likely. We asked everyone we knew to pray. Miraculously, the excess fluid largely disappeared, and I managed to make it to 38 weeks. At that point I was admitted to a large city hospital to avoid delivery in our little town. I was induced as soon as they had a delivery room, operating theatre and NICU bed all lined up at the same time. A quick and easy labor was followed by a single push and out popped a sweet little girl. After three boys in a row, I was so excited to have a girl that for a minute or two I forgot about the prospect of Down syndrome. The neonatologist was examining my baby on the other side of the room when I remembered to ask. Without answering he brought my sweet little baby over and I could see straight away the tell-tale eyes and flat nose. Without any anguish I said "Clearly, she does" and noticed the relief in the doctor's face when he realized that he wouldn't have to break the news to me. Jeff went silent beside me, and I knew that he must be aching inside. After holding her for a while I asked the nurse to cuddle our baby outside for a while. As she left, Jeff's tears began to flow, and I knew that he would have a much harder time accepting this than I would.

We had decided to name our precious girl Gianna, after Gianna Beretta Molla, a wonderful doctor who refused to abort her baby in the face of cancer and has since been canonized by the Catholic Church.

As I lay in the hospital bed that first night, I worried about how Jeff would cope. Little did I know that he spent the entire night at Gianna's side, praying for her and for God's grace to be a good father to her. When I saw him in the morning, the peace of God had filled his heart, and he, too, knew that everything was going to be fine. The two weeks Gianna spent in NICU filled me with an overwhelming desire to just take my little girl home and love and nurture her. I knew with the training I had and a loving home, Gianna would flourish and be a blessing to our family. I knew, too, that God had already given me many "normal" children to mother. This was my opportunity to experience a whole different side of motherhood. I was, indeed, blessed to be Gianna's mother. Although there is inevitable stress and frustration in raising any child, I know that God's hand is upon us and that Gianna is a wonderful part of His plan. God has since blessed us with one more little girl, Sienna, who is Gianna's best friend and built-in, round-the-clock therapist. Sienna, too, is clearly part of God's master plan.

Nicola is the mother of 7 children living on the Australian east coast. Previously a special educator, Nicola has been a stay-at-home-mother for 16 years and volunteers tutoring slow progress readers at her local school.

Chapter 30

If I Had Known

by Margaret Mary Meyers

"If you had known your children would have this gene, would you have given birth to them?" the woman across the table asked me. She was reacting to the story that one of my sons had recently become blind, while another had become legally blind several years earlier. In spite of my shock at her question, I answered with lightning speed.

"Absolutely!" I shot back. Then, sensing she expected more, I added, "They have a lot to contribute."

Paul (left) and Peter Meyers

"That's good," she said. "A lot of them just gripe." I couldn't believe this comment either. The visually impaired people I knew were wonderful, positive people. Maybe she didn't really know any.

"Because one of my sons has been legally blind for five years, I have met a lot of blind people," I said to her. "And they have a lot to contribute!"

"But if you had known, would you have had all six children?" she persisted. I responded with an emphatic yes to this, too. Later that day, I thought back to that first loss.

"What is the number of the hymn?" our youngest son, Peter, whispered to me at Mass one day, when he was 9 years old. I told him, and then I asked the other boys if they could read the number. They could—and so could he the previous week.

"He must need glasses," I thought. Both my father and my husband needed glasses at a young age. While I made an appointment for him to see an optometrist, I wasn't really worried.

"Does he have a strong desire for glasses?" the optometrist asked. None of the lenses she tried had improved his vision. She hoped he just wanted glasses so he could be like someone he admired. After I gave her an emphatic no—beginning to tremble as I realized there was something more seriously wrong here—she referred us to a specialist.

Our relatives and friends joined us in prayer for Peter. Each night as I blessed him with Lourdes water, I asked Our Blessed Mother to help him with his vision and to help him lead a happy life. By the time we visited the eye specialist, Peter could no longer read the chapter books he liked to curl up with on the couch. After a hospitalization, many different tests, and agonizing weeks of waiting for appointments and results, the doctor called us in for the diagnosis.

"Peter has something called Leber's hereditary optic neuropathy," he told us. He was sorry to tell us that there is no cure or treatment for it. He told us this gene sometimes causes damage to the optic nerve. As we researched the condition, we learned that there have been families with five or six children, where only one or two of the children have the vision loss and the others do not. Medical science has not figured out what triggers the blindness in those who have the gene. The mother passes on the gene, although it rarely affects her.

"His vision probably won't get any worse than it is now," we found out. The vision loss usually occurs within a few months. Peter is legally blind, but still has usable vision. Before Peter's vision loss, he helped his Dad with household repairs. He continued his handy-man work by teaching himself to do with his fingers what he had previously done with his eyes. He laughed about giving himself a mild shock one day, as we had heard other handymen do on occasion. He quickly learned how to plug devices in using his sense of touch, without getting shocked in the process.

One time, a year or two later, I mentioned to Peter that someone we knew had to have multiple eye surgeries and then, after all that, she still did not keep her vision. He told me that when he was in the hospital, he prayed he would not have to have eye surgery. Perhaps his guardian angel had inspired him to feel that way so he would accept the inevitability of his condition.

He had accepted his condition back when others just "knew" that there would be a cure. Lots of relatives and friends were praying. Sometimes people would tell me to pray to Saint Lucy or to Saint Barbara, and that if I had enough faith God would cure my son. I was grateful but frustrated.

"We are very grateful for the prayers and please keep them coming," I would say. "And they are being answered. God is helping Peter to accept his condition, to be close to Him, to be happy, and to move on with his life. That is the 'miracle' that we need right now and it is being granted."

These days, you can often find Peter sitting next to the television in his free time, watching football and baseball games. If Dad is not able to see a game, Peter can give him an enthusiastic description of the plays, accompanied by an extensive knowledge of the players and team standings. He plays fantasy baseball and fantasy football, keeping track of players' stats and giving advice to an older brother who also plays.

Peter spearheaded the organization of our storage unit after we relocated from Kentucky to Maryland. Even though he cannot see in detail from one end of the storage unit to the other, he mapped it all out in his head. At our homeschool group, Peter participates in social life, in the Drop of Clear Water teen functions, and in pick-up sports.

Last January, he carried the Maryland State flag in the March for Life in Washington, D.C.

For school, Peter reads print using a video magnifier, and he uses screen magnification on the computer. He can read Braille when the occasion warrants it. He is busily preparing for college, and he plans to be an accountant some day.

Life progressively returned to normal for Peter and for us—a new normal, but a happy normal. Then one day the phone rang.

"Mom," our then-college-age son Paul called from Kentucky, "I just woke up and one eye is blurry. I think I might have what Peter has." Once again, I was optimistic—or maybe I just wanted to be reassuring.

"Get to an ophthalmologist today," I said. "Maybe it's just an eye infection." But it was not an eye infection. Paul's diagnosis was the same as Peter's diagnosis had been. "The Lord gave and the Lord has taken away. Blessed be the name of the Lord," (Job 1:21 NASB) Paul quoted from Job when he talked to me after his appointment.

Paul was attending college in Northern Kentucky. We lived several hundred miles away in Baltimore. "Paul's vision loss is worse than Peter's," his older sister and brother would tell us as the days wore on. We thought they were just reacting to the shock. Surely, he just needed to learn to adapt as Peter had. Surely, his vision was no worse than Peter's.

Once again, we stormed heaven and, once again, the answer came in the form of an even stronger faith. I decided to fly out to Kentucky to accompany Paul back home for a visit. As soon as I saw him, I knew his sister and brother were right: his vision loss was severe. I swallowed my shock as we greeted one another warmly and cheerfully, and we set off to fly back to my new city.

"The deaf leading the blind," Paul and I would joke, as I led him through the airport. Because I am deaf in my right ear, he either had to use the cane in his left hand or else I could not hear what he was saying. So we played a revised form of musical chairs, switching from side to side. We laughed through the airports, enjoying life and our time together, as always.

As many times as I have flown, this was the first time that weather diverted the flight to another city. Planes did not fly from this small town to ours, so the airline said they would try to get us all a bus. Our planeload of passengers lingered through the wee hours in the baggage claim area. While we all took turns going to get food at the one shop that was still open, I was pleasantly surprised that the few complaints to airline personnel were subdued. Everyone seemed to be making an effort to be cheerful. I wondered, as I looked from Paul, sitting patiently by a pillar, to all the other passengers, if maybe they looked at him and thought, "If he can be patient, so can I." Or maybe he was praying for everyone to be at peace.

As a man of prayer with a deep faith, Paul had already joined the Newman Club, the Catholic campus ministry, on his college campus. Now he became its president. Less then a year after his vision loss occurred, Paul and others in the club made plans for Scott Hahn, popular Catholic speaker, to speak to the people of Cincinnati and Northern Kentucky. Once again, weather interfered with a flight, this time keeping Dr. Hahn in New York when he should have been arriving in Northern Kentucky. Two days later, Paul was on the telephone, busily making plans for another date, this one successful.

Throughout his college career, Paul was not only president of the Newman Club, but was also a student body senator and chancellor of his local Knights of Columbus chapter. He graduated with a chair award in his major.

Today, he writes and he speaks at youth retreats and RCIA (Rite of Christian Initiation for Adults) meetings. He cooks meals for his friends. I know that we, his many friends, and especially his lovely fiancé, are very glad that he was born! And we are very glad that Peter was born, just as we are glad that all of our children were born.

"Would you have had all six of your children if you had known you had this gene?" This question still shocks me when I think of it. I can't imagine life without any one of our beautiful children, who love life, and who bring so much joy to us and to others.

When Jesus walked the earth, He made the blind to see and the deaf to hear in order to manifest His love and His divinity. But nowhere in Scripture does it say that he cured everyone who was blind, everyone who was deaf, or everyone who had an infirmity. Our lives give glory to God, whether he cures us or whether He shines through our infirmities (and we all have infirmities, in varying degrees).

After that delayed flight with Paul, I received this email from Linda, a fellow passenger: "I have often thought of your family and how gracious your son was in adjusting to his blindness. I was so struck by his quiet determination to just move forward the best that he could. It was such a model of what Christ would have us do. May God help each of us to also model the serenity prayer (change the things we can change, accept the things we cannot change, and the wisdom to know the difference) as your son did that night."

In the Bible we read that: "As he passed by he saw a man blind from birth. His disciples asked him, 'Rabbi, who sinned, this man or his parents, that he was born blind?' Jesus answered, 'Neither he nor his parents sinned; it is so that the works of God might be made visible through him. We have to do the works of the one who sent me while it is day. Night is coming when no one can work. While I am in the world, I am the light of the world.' When he had said this, he spat on the ground and made clay with the saliva, and smeared the clay on his eyes, and said to him, 'Go wash in the Pool of Siloam' (which means Sent). So he went and washed, and came back able to see." John 9:1-7 NABRE

Each of our six children brings us great joy, but the joy they bring to God, to others, and to themselves is just as important. Most important of all is "that the works of God may be made manifest in them."

Margaret Mary Myers lives with her supportive husband and three of their six wonderful children in Baltimore, Maryland. You can find her at her blog: www.margmary.blogspot.com. You might also enjoy her son Paul's tweets twitter.com/paulsproverbs.

Gerard and Joseph Nadal

Chapter 31

An Autistic Child Shall Lead Them

by Gerard M. Nadal, Ph.D.

No Alpha-Fetoprotein (AFP) Blood Test for us, thank you all the same. This was our first child, one we had given up trying to conceive after four years of frustration. The AFP yields a frightful number of false-positive results as Regina, a pediatric nurse, and I, a graduate student of molecular biology and microbiology, knew all too well. Why bother, when resolving a positive test result would require amniocentesis, which kills one out of every 200 babies on which it is performed?

"Handicapped babies need more love, not less," we told Dr. Maggio with pro-life assurance. Then, with a flourish I slammed the door shut on any further discussion by stating, "If God has a certain number of handicapped children He needs to send into the world, we'll take one."

NEVER lay down that kind of marker before the God of the Universe unless you are prepared to follow through. I said it, and God took me up on it. Praise God that He did!

Joseph's nine months with Regina were a textbook pregnancy. My friend David, a high-risk OB/GYN, insisted on doing the sonograms. David and I go all the way back to high school and college, and I was glad to have his careful and critical eye on the baby we had despaired of ever having. On Regina's due date, Dr. Maggio saw nothing unusual and told Regina to go in for her last night of work if she wanted. The baby was riding high and had not dropped down yet. If nothing happened over the weekend (it was Thursday afternoon), he would bring Regina in on Monday and induce labor.

While Regina was at work, David called and asked for a status report. I told him there was nothing new. Then, a gravity I never heard in his voice before, David said, "Have her in the office tomorrow as soon as she gets off work." That seemed inexplicable, as the last sonogram was a week earlier and Joseph was all systems go.

In the morning, the sonogram revealed a baby who was in trouble, *very* serious trouble. Regina had reabsorbed all the amniotic fluid. The cord was wrapped around Joseph's neck. The placenta was beginning to detach. Our baby boy was dying, and David had no reason for why he sensed trouble and called the previous night. Had Regina come home from work and gone to bed, our baby would have died by the time she awoke and sensed that he was still.

Regina had an emergency C-section and Joseph was brought into the world with an ear-splitting scream, nine pounds, two ounces, and the picture of health and vitality. That night, as Regina lay in bed with a bad anesthesia reaction, compounded by pain medication, she was unaware of her surroundings. I held Joseph close in the darkened bedroom with the only light coming from the half-moon shining outside the window. We spoke a great deal that night. I praised God for the miracle of the child in my arms, and promised Joseph that I would always be there for him.

The first year was pure magic, and Joseph was developing right on schedule. He laughed and made deep eye contact. He played and giggled. He snuggled and held tightly.

Then it all started to fall apart.

The eye contact disappeared. Speech was slow in coming, with new words spoken for a few days and never heard again, interspersed by days and days of silence. Interaction with us all but vanished. He spoke no more than a few words in a sentence, and only when alone. He alternately perseverated, hand-flapped, toe-walked, fixed on spinning objects. I sensed that something was going horribly wrong, but Regina did not. That was the beginning of what was almost the end of our marriage. In short, I saw something in Joseph as broken and in need of fixing. Regina did not.

Everyone had a story about an Uncle Louie who didn't speak until the age of six and then recited the U.S. Constitution. "Boys are slower than girls." "You're an overbearing father." "Typical of a scientist; wanting a perfect child." I heard it all.

In truth, all I wanted was an average child on a normal, average developmental track.

After two years of speech therapy at Saint John's University and a private therapist, Regina insisted that I leave Joseph alone. None of the therapists suggested anything other than an expressive language delay. Nothing had worked, so I backed off after his third birthday. I seemed to be the only one who saw a major issue.

My marriage in those few years had turned toxic. I had begun to actually hate Regina for not seeing a serious problem in Joseph. Denial was fine for other people, but not in my home. Not with my son. Worst of all, the toxicity was beginning to affect our daughter Elizabeth, who was born when Joseph was 18 months old. Beth began to throw tantrums so wild that her voice began to sound husky, like a three-pack-a-day smoker. Then came a third child, little Regina, amidst toxic resentments so bad that Regina and I agreed one night that our marriage was over.

God yelled rather pointedly in my head to fix this, NOW! I got off the couch an hour after we agreed to divorce and went to our room. "We're not getting a divorce!!" I yelled at Regina.

"Fine!!" she yelled back. And so we began to walk back slowly from the brink.

Joseph's Pre-K school director was the first to suggest that he might be on the autism spectrum. After grabbing every book I could find at Borders and Barnes and Noble, I researched the best autism experts in the nation and miraculously got Joseph evaluated at the University of Michigan's Autism Center and Columbia University's Pediatric Neurology department. We also got him a comprehensive speech evaluation by a crack therapist in Albany, NY. Then came the shattering diagnoses:

Autism, ADHD, mixed expressive/receptive language disorder, static encephalopathy, cerebellar deficit. A month shy of his fifth birthday, Joseph's age equivalent in speech was 2.1 years. His I.Q. test sub scores placed him at low average to borderline retarded. Reflexively, I took it all to prayer.

"I said I would take a handicapped child, but you need to hold up your end of the bargain," I said as I knelt before the Blessed Sacrament day after day. I told God that I needed a special education teacher for 10 hours per week at home, and one with a background in speech therapy. I needed a woman who could speak the same language as Regina and coordinate the follow-through at home for all of Joseph's therapies.

I came home on day seven to a message from a pre-med student I had met almost two years earlier, Mary Szabo. Mary, the daughter of a married couple who taught at St. John's University, wanted me to work with her privately for the Medical College Admission Test. As we discussed her educational background, it came to light that Mary had done pre-med studies after her M.S. degree in special education (She was then working with autistic toddlers!) Her B.S. was in speech therapy!

Mary became a part of our family for the next two years and hit it off with Regina from the outset. We owe her far more than the pre-med work I did with her. Mary was the catalyst for the healing between Regina and me. Mary helped me to understand the pain in a mother's heart, the reflexive self-blame that often accompanies disability and frequently leads to denial as a defense mechanism.

At the center of the therapy was a brilliant speech therapist that has become like a brother to me, Mr. Robert Marinello. Bob has the reputation, after more than 35 years, of being a miracle worker with autistic children. Joseph responded well to Bob from the very first day, and now, seven years later, people ask us if he could have been misdiagnosed.

Another part of the success with Joseph came when I reverted to my training as a clinical professor. "We treat the patient before us, not the textbook," I tell my students. Regina and I agreed to use the diagnoses only as a tool to point toward the most efficacious therapies. And so we began.

Joseph is still shy and retiring and takes some time to warm up to others. However, he joined a bowling league two years ago and in his first year won the United States Bowling Congress bronze medal for boys, ages 11 and under, in New York State. The next year he won the triple-crown trophy for high game, high average and high series. Joseph has been doing Irish step dancing for four years, as well as jazz and tap, and is a natural. He recently joined the Boy Scouts. He achieved his first rank and is rapidly advancing to his second rank. He's also a straight-A student, altar boy, and catcher on the fifth grade baseball team for our parish (I'm his coach), playing since kindergarten.

Like the many other boys I've met who live life on the autism spectrum, Joseph is sweet and kind, and actually very sensitive. It isn't that affection and emotion are impossible, as so many think. They simply need to be taught with an extra measure of diligence and patience.

Our entire home life has been transformed by Joseph's needs. So has our marriage. When all social skills and communication skills need to be hand-wired, instead of allowed to naturally unfold as occurs in 'normal' children, you're forced to pause and listen to what the people around you are saying.

I quit my career in teaching and pulled our children from our parish school in order to home school them, when Joseph was being verbally abused and educationally neglected by his third grade teacher. The administration did nothing about such bullying, rampant in the school. Homeschooling has been the greatest blessing for the children and our family.

He may never know it, but Joseph has taught us more about God's love, about spousal love, about the beauty of life than we have or ever will teach him. We have no idea what the future holds for Joseph. He has two sisters who love him, and whom he loves in return, and they will walk life's road together.

As a scientist, I fear that we will soon identify common genetic markers that will be used to screen and abort babies with autism. With as many as one in 80 children on the spectrum, that is an appalling increase in abortions. The truth about special children is that they transform our lives for the better. We are here to learn how to love, as Dostoevsky stated in *The Brothers Karamazov*:

"Brothers, love is a teacher, but one must know how to acquire it, for it is hard to acquire, it is dearly bought, it is won by long labor. For we must love not only occasionally, but forever."

In this, Joseph has been my greatest professor.

Dr. Nadal holds a B.A. in Psychology, an M.S. in Cellular and Molecular Biology, a Master of Philosophy in Biology, and Ph.D. in Molecular Microbiology. Dr. Nadal studied for a year in Seminary.

He has taught science at Saint John's University, and, Manhattan College.

Dr Nadal is editor and columnist at the Center for Morality in Public Life, and writes for Headline Bistro, Life Site News, and Life News.

A speaker on the life issues, Dr Nadal has also been a guest on radio shows, including The Janet Parshall Show and The Drew Mariani Show. Currently Dr. Nadal is director of Medical Students for Life of America, and is leading an autism research project, and pursuing an M.A. in Theology through Franciscan University.

Craig and Heidi Saxton, Christopher and Sarah

Chapter 32

The Woman in the Mirror

by Heidi Hess-Saxton

One morning when you least expect it, you'll look in the mirror and find it looking back at you. The phantasm bears a slight resemblance to your familiar self, except... Is it possible that your husband installed a trick mirror while you were dozing, just for kicks? This gal has...

Eyes bloodshot from getting up every two hours with one toddler's night terrors and the other's asthma attacks.

Stomach is rumbling from not eating a decent meal since... What is this? May?

Throat is raw from screaming like a fishwife, just to hear herself above the din.

In the same set of sweats she's worn all week, sans bra. Even to the doctor's office.

And as the bathroom door reverberates with the pounding of three insistent sets of little fists, you pray the lock will hold long enough for you to sit down for five seconds and have one coherent thought.

Suddenly, it hits you:

This is not what I signed up for. I don't recognize that ghoulish figure in the mirror. She's grouchy. She's wrinkled and rumpled, and so are her clothes. She smells like baby barf. Make her go away.

Easier said than done. But if you watch my back, and I watch yours, maybe we can figure this out together. We'll get those Mommy Monsters.

TAMING THE MOMMY MONSTER

In my book *Raising Up Mommy* I write about the seven deadly sins of motherhood – and the "celestial virtues" we need to acquire as an antidote to those spiritually toxic habits.

The thing is, I never realized how desperately I needed them until I became a mother. Didn't realize how angry, selfish, and miserly I could be with those I professed to love most. In retrospect, I've come to believe that it was because *God* knew precisely these things about me, He sent these particular children my way.

I'd like to say that in a short time, I had eradicated all traces of self-centeredness and sloth from my soul. That wouldn't be true. But in the words of the old hymn by Annie J. Flint,

> "He giveth more grace as the burdens grow greater,
> he sendeth more strength as the labors increase.
> To added afflictions, he addeth more mercy,
> To multiplied trials his multiplied peace.

His love hath no limit, his grace hath no measure
His love hath no boundaries known unto men.
But out of the infinite riches of Jesus,
He giveth, and giveth, and giveth again."

LIVING WITH THE HARD CHOICES

One of the hardest lessons I had to learn was recognizing my own limits, and doing what was right rather than what was popular.

When the children first came to us, there were three of them. Within a few weeks, it became clear that three was one too many; because of what they had endured prior to coming into care; they needed more attention than I could possibly give them on my own.

After about a year, we asked the social worker to find another placement for the oldest child – someplace where there were no other small children, and she could have the undivided attention she needed. Our intention was to raise the children like cousins, seeing one another for birthdays and holidays and day trips. We recognized this wasn't ideal – but we also recognized that, in this situation, it was all we could do.

In retrospect, it was absolutely the right choice. Their sister flourished in her new home, and grew up to be a beautiful, thoughtful young woman. Every time we see her, we thank God for bringing that couple into her life – and every time, we reassure ourselves that we did indeed make the right choice for all of us.

It wasn't the popular choice. People who knew us only casually were horrified to learn that the girl was going to live somewhere else. How could we abandon the child like this, making it impossible for her to trust anyone again? How could we just give up on her?

It wasn't easy. In fact, it was humiliating. But it was the right thing to do.

That is the beauty of adoption. For every "impossible" child, God has prepared his parents, giving them just the right graces in just the right amount (though sometimes those qualities are latent until they have a chance to be exercised a bit!) so that they can help one another to Heaven. It's never easy – neither the letting go, nor the welcoming. But the graces are there for the taking. Jesus said it best: "And who ever receives one child such as this in my name receives me." Matt 18:5 NABRE

Heidi Hess Saxton is an author of several books including Raising Up Mommy and Behold Your Mother. The foster-adoptive mother of two children with emotional and learning disability, Heidi blogs for parents of adopted, foster and special needs children at the "Extraordinary Moms Network." You can reach her at Heidi.hess.saxton@gmail.com.

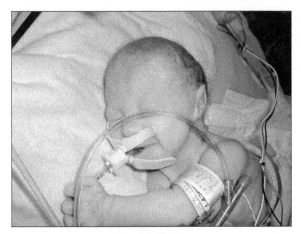

Rita McGuire

Chapter 33

The Little Girl Who Lived a Novena

by Colleen McGuire

I thought that I had done my part. As the mother of 11 children, with another on the way, I felt that my family was a humble witness to the sanctity of life. But God called us to greater sacrifice with the pregnancy and birth of our 12th child in late 2004 and early 2005.

That was the year Terri Schiavo's parents fought for her life, and Blessed John Paul II showed us all what it means to offer up your body in sacrifice to God. As I laid on an examination table for my 11-week sonogram, I was barely aware of the growing fury over Schiavo's care or the growing pain of our Holy Father. And yet their examples would prove invaluable for me and my family as our baby struggled for life.

A technician performed that 11-week sonogram at a high-risk obstetrician's office, and I gave blood for a screening test for genetic abnormalities. Although I had never had any of these tests before, I felt that at 44, they might bring me some peace of mind. The results showed no sign of Down syndrome, which was my main concern. But the doctor did say that there was an elevation with regards to another trisomy disorder, and recommended a follow-up sonogram at 22 weeks. Thinking that the elevation was a fluke, I put the results out of my mind.

As a high-risk obstetrician began this second sonogram 11 weeks later, I naively asked whether I was having a boy or girl. He looked straight at me and said, "I think that's the least of your worries." He went on to tell me in a cold, clinical way that my results indicated a high possibility of trisomy 18. As a registered nurse, I knew this meant that there are three copies of the 18th chromosome. He began to list the problems my baby could have: major heart abnormalities, spina bifida, severe neurological and developmental problems, hearing loss, and more. Many die in utero, during birth or within days of birth.

"You have a lot to think about here," the doctor continued matter-of-factly. "You're already at 22 weeks."

"If you mean termination of pregnancy, I won't do that," I said. "So, you can forget about it." He did advise me to have an amniocentesis in order to confirm the diagnosis. I went into the ladies room and cried alone. I asked God if I would be able to handle this. I prayed, "Dear Lord, if this is to be, please help me to accept it and go on."

I got dressed and met the doctor in his office. He told me that he scheduled me for the amniocentesis, in case I changed my mind. That is when I started to waver. I actually considered the invasive test, which causes death in less than 1 percent of babies, according to the American College of Obstetricians and Gynecologists. I thought that I might feel better if we had a definitive diagnosis. When I arrived home, I called my husband, Kieran, and shared the news and my feelings. His calm words reassured me.

"You know, Colleen," he said, "There is a risk of miscarriage with this test. We don't want to lose this child that way. What are we going to do if the baby has this problem? We are going to accept the baby anyway, as he or she is, and deal with it, right?" When I agreed, he went on. "Just cancel the appointment; we don't need an amniocentesis. We'll love this child and have him or her baptized. That's how we'll do this."

From then on, our goal became a simple one: to help our baby be born alive and baptized into our Catholic faith. We lined up all the people we knew to pray for this intention. Then we chose St. Rita of Cascia as her patroness. I had visited the Shrine of St. Rita in Philadelphia a few months earlier, before we were aware of the baby's problems. St. Rita, along with St. Jude, is the patron of impossible causes. I read her story at the shrine and found it to be amazing. She had suffered through the murders of her husband and sons, and later became a nun.

Before I even knew about the trisomy 18, I had decided that if I had a girl I would name her Rita. When I found out she had trisomy 18, I said, "St. Rita, you are the patroness of impossible causes. Allow my child to be born alive so that we can baptize her; we will take care of her. Please get me through the pregnancy." So, St. Rita became my number-one intercessor, though many of my friends were praying to St Gerard Majella, patron of expectant women. It was a wonderful experience, an opportunity to ask for prayers, and I was amazed when I found out how many people were praying for us.

Our first hurdle on this journey toward birth came when we considered that many babies with trisomy 18 die during labor because the process is too stressful for their fragile bodies. I decided to have a C-section, and our regular obstetrician was supportive. The high-risk obstetrician, however, initially refused, given the risks and my age. I explained that I had already had one C-section and felt confident that I could handle another. We had quite an argument before he finally agreed. "You know, people are going to think you're crazy," he said coldly. That was fine with us, I assured him.

During this time, we were also able to connect with other families of children with trisomy 18. One woman, who lived near me on Long Island, had a daughter who lived for a month. She had formed an apostolate through a hospital social worker to help other mothers. She listened to my story and told that I needed to form a birth plan. She said that we had to decide how we wanted the birth to go. Did we want a priest there to baptize the baby? Did we want the best medical team there in case of a crisis?

"You didn't have an amnio, so you're not even sure what she's dealing with," she explained. "So, the hospital will probably have the neo-natal team there." Our choice to protect our baby from the dangers of amniocentesis had actually worked to our advantage: because the doctors weren't sure that our baby had trisomy 18, they would have to be prepared for any scenario. They couldn't simply send the OB and a few nurses, arguing that our baby would not survive very long anyway. A blood test to confirm trisomy 18 would take several days, during which they would have to give our child all the care they would give any "normal" baby.

Despite the pessimistic prognosis we received from the doctors, I learned that some babies survive long beyond birth. I spoke with a mother whose daughter was 7 years old. From her, I learned of other children who had defied the odds. This meant that we had to do more in-depth research into the medical needs of children with trisomy 18—and how to best care for them.

We settled into a new routine of praying and preparing for week 38, when my high-risk obstetrician would perform the C-section. At week 37, however, I had another sonogram to check the baby's measurements and amniotic fluid levels. When I arrived home, I received a phone call telling me to come in the next day. My amniotic fluid was dangerously low and they had to deliver the baby a week early.

I was nervous, but at peace. I knew that God was watching over us, and I felt confident that our baby would indeed be born alive and baptized into the Church. Our priest friend Fr. Nichols was able to come early to be with us and perform the ceremony. This was a great consolation. Even the manner of our obstetrician—the one who had initially opposed the C-section—had changed from our earlier encounter. He treated us warmly as we arrived at the hospital and seemed quite touched when Fr. Nichols gave me a blessing in Latin before the procedure began.

"What the heck is going on here," he asked in surprise. "You have your own priest?"

Rita was born at just over three pounds, with good color and a healthy cry. She did have spina bifida, and her legs were in a deformed position, with the soles of her feet facing each other like hands in prayer. Her heart was perfectly normal, and she was breathing on her own. We were hopeful that our little girl would defy the odds. She was obviously a fighter.

On day two, the neurosurgeon operated on Rita to close up her spine, so that she would not be exposed to infection. She did very well, and again we were hopeful. I was discharged from the hospital, the first time in 12 births that I went home without my baby. I was an emotional wreck, but I felt physically strong and experienced no complications from the C-section. That was a great blessing because I was able to devote all my energy to little Rita.

The amazing thing that I noticed, as her mother, was that she seemed aware of me. She would grab my pinky finger in her tiny hand and put on what I would call a smile. Before doctors had to insert the breathing tube down her throat, Rita would make cooing noises when I visited. It was such a consolation to know that she recognized me as her mother; she even seemed to recognize Kieran's voice.

The next seven days were difficult. When the genetic tests came back positive for trisomy 18, we met with the doctors to determine a plan of care for Rita. She had begun to experience difficulty breathing and had to be intubated repeatedly. This obviously caused her great distress, but she could not function long without the ventilator. The oxygen mask alone was not enough to keep her oxygen levels high. In addition, Rita was receiving food through a tube in her nose because she could not suck. We could see that her body was slowly shutting down.

We did not want Rita to suffer unnecessarily, so we called a moral theologian we knew at St. Joseph's Seminary, also known as Dunwoodie, in Yonkers, NY. He assured us that we did not have to maintain this level of care for her because she had a condition that was incompatible with life. But I like to say that her condition was compatible with Eternal Life because she was going to Heaven sooner than any of us. We were going to have our own St. Rita! She was going to be free of pain and bodily deformities. We were at peace with our decision to let her return to God.

We knew then that we had to gather all our children, some of whom were away at school. Everybody needed to arrive home so that we could spend time together as a family, loving her as much as we could until the moment of her passing. The children had not yet met their little sister because she was in the neo-natal intensive care unit. We spoke with the social worker about arranging a private room, where we could spend time together. She was completely supportive and arranged everything.

When Kieran brought the children to the hospital, it was all so natural. Each of them took a turn holding their little sister and getting to know her. Some of them cried quietly as she opened her eyes and looked at them. They were amazed at how tiny she was—such a peanut! After several hours, the children were growing tired. Since we didn't know how much longer Rita would be with us, Kieran brought them home. Then he returned to keep watch with me.

We spent the rest of the hours she remained on earth holding her and loving her. We knew that it was the last day of her life because the nurses were preparing us. We took turns holding her until the end, but it was only the beginning, really. I would never deny anybody the opportunity to assist their child into Heaven. We felt as if we were standing at the foot of the Cross, but we knew it was a gift to hold her in our arms. Rita did not give in easily and kept looking at us with her beautiful eyes. I kept saying to her, "You will know how much you are loved. You may not know it right now, but you will know soon how much we loved you." That is what got me through my own little Calvary.

When Rita finally returned to God, my husband insisted that we bring her home. A local funeral parlor agreed to hold the wake in our house. When the little casket arrived, family, friends, and neighbors began knocking on the door. We were not sure how our children would react, but we needn't have worried. One by one, they approached the casket, knelt down and started to pray. We had explained to them that she was a saint because she was baptized and totally innocent. I will never forget how my son Kieran took off his scapular, rubbed it to Rita's skin, and said, "I now have a second-class relic!" Then five other children decided to make their own relics with various items. It really was a wonderful experience. I can say for certain that I do not regret bringing Rita home. Her presence there brought peace to our family.

Since we live down the block from our parish church, we brought Rita there in procession, singing hymns as we went. Neighbors came out and watched us; it was a real witness to the Faith. As we entered the church, I caught my breath: it was packed! We had not really spread the word about Rita's Mass, but somehow people knew. We never realized how many of our friends and neighbors had been praying for us. What a testimony to our Faith and the ways in which we, as the Body of Christ, uplift each other. We need each other. What a consolation their presence was!

The ceremony was a beautiful Mass of the Angels because, as Fr. Nichols explained, it is not considered a funeral if you know the person is definitely in Heaven. After he had celebrated this Missa de Angelis, the traditional Mass in Latin, he said that he was honored. "This is my first Mass for a saint!" he exclaimed.

Afterwards, life went on and people would come to me and say, "I've been praying for your daughter's intercession." A year later, a young man who attends school with my son said, "You know, I pray to her every day." This young man had traveled from school with my sons to attend Rita's Mass, and it made a real impression on him.

It was humbling to hear people's thoughts about Rita. I would think, "Who am I to be the mother of a saint? Do I deserve this honor?"

All I can say to any mother who receives a frightening diagnosis is that you don't know what will happen—but God does. Your faith and trust in Him will see you through anything. I know a woman who lost her baby to the same diagnosis, and she told me, "You know, it was such a privilege. This child had such an impact on so many people." That's how you have to look at it. These children make their impact in ways you may not even be aware of.

In addition to the many people who have prayed for Rita's intercession, I heard much later that our little girl touched the high-risk obstetrician who initially seemed so cold and opposed to our plan to bring her safely into this world. A colleague of his later told me that even now, years later, he continues to ask about our family. During Rita's hospital stay, various nurses and medical personnel would come into my room and tell us that we did the right thing by bringing her into the world. We could see the impact she had on them. One of the doctors from our OB's practice, who is originally from Africa, listened intently as I told him about our decision to have a C-section. "You did the perfect thing," he told me. "You did what was right, absolutely. You did not make an error in judgment. Look at this beautiful baby you brought into this world!"

The effect on my own family has been tremendous. We no longer take our life together for granted. We know that we have to help each other and to appreciate every day we have together. God gave us Rita for a reason, and we still feel intimately connected with her. My two youngest daughters, Mary and Helen, were only 2 and 4 years old when Rita was born. After her death, Helen would cry, "I miss Rita; I want Rita to be here with us."

I would tell her, "I know that you miss her. But God has a plan. His plan was for her to be here with us for a short time and then go to Heaven. Right now, she's there, helping us in ways we don't even know."

I truly believe that Rita helped our family to understand and appreciate the Mystical Body of Christ, my children's relationship with each other, and how special they really are. You're the youngest for a reason, or you're the middle child for a reason. God does not make mistakes. He did not make a mistake with Rita, and we were privileged to be part of her life. I know that Rita knew us. She knew her siblings; she heard their voices. She knew that she was loved, and that has helped us through our loss. She remains a member of our family, and we will continue to ask for her intercession. I don't regret one moment of her life. My daughter lived a novena: nine days of love.

Colleen McGuire lives with her family on Long Island, NY.

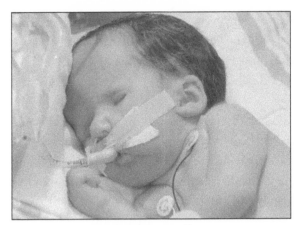
Naomi Rose Coffin

Chapter 34

"Grace at the Heart of Grief"

by Patrick Coffin

This is the story of how "God came to our assistance and made haste to help us."(Liturgy of the Hours/Psalm 69 NASB) amid the one trial every parent fears most. And He did so using ordinary events, people, and a striking series of coincidences. G.K. Chesterton called coincidences "spiritual puns," an insight as absorbing as it is relevant to our story. I'll use only the first names of those involved.

Our first two girls, Mariclare, 4, and Sophia, 20 months, were born healthy, precocious, and happy. My wife, Mariella, and I wanted more little members on Team Coffin, so when we learned of number three, our refrigerator was happily bedecked with early ultrasound images framed between to-do lists and Crayola masterpieces. Like most parents of rambunctious kids, we took it for granted that all would be sweetness and light.

"THERE'S SOMETHING WRONG WITH THE BABY."

Things soon turned sour and dark when Mariella's doctor found an anomaly in the baby's tiny 12-week-old brain, along with some other signs that were described ominously as "unwelcome."

"There's something wrong with the baby," Mariella told me that night, not quite able to hide tears. My husbandly bromides, "Don't worry, Honey," and "Doctors aren't always right," fell pancake flat. A specialist asked for another ultrasound.

On Divine Mercy Sunday, we sat drenched in worry when we glanced up at the cherished honeymoon photo of Pope John Paul II holding our hands in his. We promised him our prayers and asked for his. It seemed fitting to pray the nine-day Divine Mercy Chaplet of St. Faustina, John Paul's fellow Pole who was canonized by him in 2000. Despite the daily chaplet, I found myself unable to concentrate at work and became easy prey to crying jags. I'd be sitting at a red light when suddenly my eyeballs felt like loose valves losing a battle against a gushing fire hydrant. Dads are hardwired to protect their children, especially the vulnerable ones. Here I could protect nothing.

Reaching out to us, our next-door neighbor Roz gave Mariella a Miraculous Medal that had touched the stigmata bandages of St. Padre Pio. Mariella took it to subsequent medical exams, the first of which was that dreaded ultrasound. It fell the day after the chaplet ended.

The lights were dimmed, and wobbly images of our baby flickered in the near dark, accompanied by a litany of scary medical jargon: The baby's lateral ventricles were dilated; the finger positions and overall cranial shape were abnormal; the heart was surrounded by fluid and presented a ventricular septal defect, otherwise known as a hole. We heard the words "bad sign" a dozen times in five minutes. All indications pointed to trisomy 18, a rare and lethal genetic condition. I sat passively, holding my wife's hand, pretending I wasn't really hearing what I was hearing. Questions percolated, and not without anger: Hadn't we prayed that this would turn out to be only a scare? Doesn't God answer all prayers? Our other kids are in great health—why not this one?

LIFE TAKES LETTING GO

The monitor was switched off, and any hope to which I was clinging drained out of me like gold dust through a prospector's fingers. Staring at the dead monitor, I half heard my wife tell me she had to go to the restroom and the doctor tell me to step into a nearby meeting room. I drifted ghostlike into the room with surreal images of our broken baby branded in my mind's eye.

As I stepped toward the window and peered into the harsh noontime sunlight, waves of panic and dread, heartache, and the unremitting feeling that things were going to get terrifyingly worse—all of it stormed my ramparts. I shut my eyes tight, stood almost vibrating with grief, and stabbed at some semblance of a prayer for a sign of God's presence.

Opening my eyes, I saw an absurdly large billboard angled straight at the window a block away. Blinking away tears, I could see a father and child holding hands jumping off a small cliff into a glittering lake. On the left, in bold letters, the billboard announced, "LIFE TAKES LETTING GO."

My soul was flooded with an unearthly consolation, as though the hurt was taken from the pain. I almost started laughing. Those jumbo words made me see that most of the hurt was rooted in my unwillingness to give my child over to the care of her true Father. Clinging tightly to that little baby, grasping desperately at strategies by which I could control things, I had spiritually strangled myself. Letting go was precisely what I dreaded most. But Life Himself seemed to be telling me that this was the best thing, the only thing, to be done. Talk about the divine sense of humor: I ask for a sign, I get a billboard.

As unlikely as it seems, that brief moment switched some inner default setting from Belief to Trust. As my friend Ross, a clinical psychologist, reminded me, believing in God is not identical to trusting in Him. It's one thing to talk piously about being at the foot of the Cross, another to carry it, and still another to hang on it.

Amniocentesis was strongly advised, and we reluctantly agreed. While we normally prefer not to know our babies' sex beforehand, we made an exception, found out it was a little girl, and promptly named her Naomi Rose. The results also brought news that sent our hopes soaring—the doctor was wrong about it being the death-dealing trisomy 18. Rather, Naomi's ninth pair of chromosomes had a small extra portion of chromosomal material, a condition known as partial trisomy 9q, partial monosomy 9p. Only a few hundred cases are extant since being identified in 1973.

I relayed the way God was making His presence known to us—especially the billboard business—to my friend Chris, whom I had first met at his wedding nine years before. Chris urged me to write it all down. I didn't realize that God was just getting started in the help department, nor that my former boss and mentor, Lisa, was praying that God would send us signs of His presence.

Spring gave way to summer, and summer faded into fall. I peppered my blog with updates on her condition and readers continued to flood me with pledges of prayer, support, and encouragement. Word spread and strangers from near and far began checking in on Naomi's progress. Mariella's obstetrician, Dr. Thomas, a practicing Catholic and father of nine, gave us a vial of holy water from Lourdes. Such gestures of support and empathy were overwhelming.

OUR LADY OF TRIUMPH

Since Naomi persisted in breech position, she had to debut by C-section, which was scheduled for Thursday, September 13. A quick glance at the liturgical calendar showed that this was the memorial of Our Lady of Sorrows.Oh, great, I thought. Bad omen. Days after, owing to a scheduling glitch, the surgery was pushed to the next day, September 14, the Feast of the Triumph of the Cross, which fell on a Friday. The great Archbishop Fulton Sheen once wrote that "nothing ever happens out of heaven except with a finesse of all details." In a lovely example of such finesse, Naomi's birth was set for 3 pm, the hour of mercy, on a Friday, on the Feast of the Triumph of the Cross. I wept.

Nature wept, too. September 14 brought the first rain in months. I went to morning Mass primed to hear some uplifting words on the glories of Christ's victory, but our good pastor, Fr. Ed, mistakenly prepared an instructive homily on Our Lady of Sorrows. One must guard against over-interpreting random events, but this struck me as a sign that the Blessed

Mother, who knew a thing or two about having a child in trouble, was walking with us.

Mariella and I headed to Hollywood Presbyterian/Queen of Angels Hospital, where a team of top-flight specialists awaited Naomi's arrival. As she emerged into the light, what is normally a mother's cup of blessing was for Mariella a chalice full of anxiety. An eerie silence attended Naomi's birth. After the breathing ventilator was inserted, the tiny bundle Mariella carried beneath her heart for nine months had to be whisked next door to Children's Hospital of Los Angeles, a most wrenching separation for her mother.

The same questions raced through our minds: Would Naomi be a special needs baby (our best-case scenario)? Was this illness the start of some lifelong cross we were being asked to carry? Was this parting only a rehearsal for a worse good-bye?

Our particular prayer to John Paul the Great was to resolve Naomi's septal defect so we could meet her face-to-face. At birth, the hole was nowhere in sight. That evening I baptized her with the Lourdes water. Two days later, Fr. Ed made her a full member of the Church through Confirmation. Father showed me the old Latin/English prayer book he had dusted off to find the Rite of Confirmation for Baptized Children. The Latin inscription commemorating its approval in 1947 by Pope Pius XII was dated September 14, Naomi's day of birth. Another spiritual pun to make Chesterton proud.

On Mariclare's birthday, September 23, which happens to be the feast day of St. Padre Pio, I laid the blessed relic on Naomi's forehead and asked that through his intercession, God's perfect will would be done in her life. In seconds she began to stir. I came around to the other side of her bed and was stunned to see two milky blue eyes staring up at me. After nine slumber-like days, Naomi blessed us with a silent hello.

ALL TIME IS BORROWED

Poignant for us was how beautiful Naomi became with each passing day. We had braced ourselves for the sight of misshapen ears, facial abnormalities—the whole works. And while at birth she showed clear signs of something being "off," despite the tubes, tapes, and wires, not a day went by that we didn't use the use the word "angel" to describe her.

My parents and sister arrived from Nova Scotia, and Mariella's mother came from Peru some days later. The extended family settled into a daily ritual of visits for as long as the NICU rules allowed, many of which were bent for us. Unspoken as it was, we knew these bittersweet visitations couldn't go on indefinitely.

A neonatal MRI brought us the can't-turn-back news. One of the head doctors, Dr. Claire, strode into the room, and I turned to introduce myself. Even before she spoke, a determined, sorrowful look in her eye drilled straight into me, telegraphing a single brute fact: Naomi was going to die.

Dr. Claire herself was very pregnant, and as she described the severity and finality of our daughter's condition, she unconsciously stroked her belly as if to protect her baby from the news. Speaking in clipped, nervous tones, Dr. Claire pronounced that Naomi was not a candidate for any form of curative intervention. Her little heart still had a dangerous flaw called a coarctation, or narrowing, of the artery leading out of the heart. The drug used to treat it was only delaying the inevitable, and she would never be able to breathe on her own. Her brain ventricles were also catastrophically enlarged and her basal ganglia were riddled with necrosis. In layman's terms, her brain couldn't run her body.

It fell to us to decide the hour of our baby's death. Sharing our fears with Dr. Thomas, he emphasized that ending extraordinary treatment would not be the cause of her death—that job was taken by trisomy 9. Whether one lasts 75 hours or 75 years, he was saying, we are each equally in God's hands. For every man, all time is borrowed.

More days drifted by as we resisted accepting the unacceptable. We consulted magisterial documents related to end-of-life issues, prayed like never before, and discussed the matter with the chaplain, a faithful young priest named Fr. John. Upon meeting, Father and I recognized each other but neither could place from where. I mentioned this to Chris, who chided my memory lapse. I had indeed met Fr. John before: He'd witnessed Chris's and his wife's marriage vows nine years before.

Meeting our 4-year-old for the first time, Fr. John reached into his valise and said, "Mariclare, I've been wondering who to give this to, and now I know," as he handed her a lovely rosewood rosary that had been blessed by Pope John Paul in Paris. Its central bead was a round silver image of a monk. I took a closer look. Padre Pio's grinning face looked back.

Having been told Naomi would soon be going to heaven, we asked Mariclare if she had any questions about anything at all. She looked at Fr. John and gave us a much-needed toddler moment. "Yes," she said without guile. "Will Jesus be able to juggle Naomi with all the other babies?"

AN ANGEL TO CHARM THE ARCHANGELS

We picked the Feast of the Archangels, September 29. Her death would also fall on a Friday. Each family member kissed her good-bye, and Fr. John administered the Anointing of the Sick for a last strengthening.

Providentially, a no-nonsense Catholic nurse named Katy was on duty that morning. At our request, Katy began the tube disconnections at noon, mirroring the start of Our Lord's crucifixion. As she was freed at last from the bed, facial tape, and sundry tubes, we drank in Naomi's delicate beauty for the first, last, and only time. Extra doses of pain medication were introduced and for the next two hours Mariella and I gently passed her back and forth between us, covered her with kisses, whisper-sang "Twinkle Twinkle Little Star," and wet her hair with our tears.

But those moments had none of the previous qualities of angst and depression. On the contrary, we felt quite carried along by many peoples' prayers, and we knew with the certainty of faith that Our Lord would soon take Naomi from our arms to His. Her room took on the aspect of a sacred chapel. Most people enter the kingdom of God as babies; very few get three sacraments en route to glory as Naomi did in her 15 days on earth. St. Thomas Aquinas taught that the suffering of innocents, along with death itself, comprises the greatest obstacle to belief in God. Naomi manifested both. Is it not by looking to the innocent Christ suffering and dying on the Cross that we can "resolve" that terrible mystery by continuing to trust?

Naomi's little life continues to have a big impact. We pray to her constantly. Trials like losing a child can bring untold blessings and a new tolerance for the "small things" that used to loom so important. My father coined the phrase "Naomi strikes again" to indicate a prayer answered or a grace received. She's brought deeper bonds between family members, healing of lapsed friendships, new wonderment at the power of intercessory prayer, and a visceral appreciation for life's fragility. Paradoxically, our inner selves feel more solid.

St. Faustina once wrote: "Receive into the abode of Your Most Compassionate Heart all meek and humble souls and the souls of little children. These souls send all heaven into ecstasy and they are the heavenly Father's favorites." In that spirit, our family recommends asking mighty Naomi to put in a good word.

For being juggled by Jesus has its privileges.

Reprinted with permission from the Jan/Feb 2007 issue of Lay Witness magazine. © 2011 Catholics United for the Faith www.cuf.org

Patrick Coffin writes from Los Angeles. He is an author and radio host at Catholic Answers Live. Patrick blogs at http://seizethedei.blogspot.com

Chapter 35

Letter to a Special Needs Mother

MY DEAR SISTER IN CHRIST,

Like me, you have questioned God's gift of a special needs child. Please know that He loves you deeply, and knows you intimately, better than you know yourself. His love for you is infinite; however, He desires to make you holier and more loving by drawing you closer to Himself. This can only be done by purifying you, as He did with the children of Israel. He led them to purification through fire. Fire purifies gold by burning off the impurities. Having your desires for a healthy baby "ignored" by God is His way of helping you let go and trust Him to re-shape your idea of happiness. Happiness in the world's eyes is prosperity and health, peace and smooth sailing. As you have read in His Word, His ways are not our ways.

If you read the lives of God's closest friends, the saints, you will see how often He said "no" to their perfectly reasonable desires. They suffered disease, poverty, persecutions—and sometimes this left them feeling abandoned by God. Yet He loved them so much that He wanted to kiss them from the Cross, allowing them to share His Son's suffering, and, by offering their suffering united with His to share in the work of saving souls. Sometimes, it can be hard to bear. You are in good company; Mother Teresa once said, "Tell Jesus He can stop kissing me so much!"

You have been called by Our Lord to a unique and noble vocation: to raise a special needs child. This requires that you put your entire trust in Him in order to overcome your fear of having a child whom the world deems incomplete. To go against the current of popular opinion which says that a disabled baby is the worst thing that can happen to a family. Did you know that 92 percent of mothers who received news like your child's diagnosis aborted their children? You have already proven that you are one of the elite 8 percent who said "yes" to life. God is so proud of you!

Now He wants you to learn a higher level of trust by going against your natural reaction to infirmity and your maternal fears for your child's future. You will struggle with this, for example, when you see your daughter's development lagging behind her typical classmates, or when you worry about what your son will do for a living. Learning to trust God is a lifelong process, and it usually hurts.

Soon you will notice that you have an increased capacity to love, as you learn to love God for who He is, not for what He does for you—even if you do so while gritting your teeth. When you can act in loving ways even when you don't feel like it—caring for your child when you are upset or feel like you have no time for yourself or your other children—you are growing in love. That is the goal of your life-long walk with God.

This gift can seem very strange indeed, but you must remember that this increased capacity for love will surpass your expectations. Perhaps you did not think you could cope with a special needs child. However, as each challenge appears, you will find that Our Lord will not abandon you in this very special mission. He wants you to accept this child as a gift from His Hand, as Mary accepted the gift of Jesus, trusting the future to His loving Providence.

Are you worried about your child's future? He holds that in His Hands, too. This is a fear you overcome, little by little, as you see every stage of development happen, like watching a slow-motion film of a rose unfolding. And each accomplishment will mean so much more to you. I promise that someday soon you will look back on these dark days as Our Lady did; you will ponder the mystery of your special child in your heart with wonder and deep gratitude.

You will have peace again, more than you ever experienced before. Peace that can never be shattered by circumstances. Peace deep in your soul, peace in knowing God loves you and ultimately works all things for the good of those who love Him. Peace that He holds in his hands a wonderful future for you and your child: eternal union with Him in Heaven.

However, He cannot complete this work without frequent communication with you. So, you need to receive His grace regularly through the sacraments. You also need support from family and friends. Pray every day. Ask your spouse and your children to pray for their new brother or sister. This is a good time to get in the habit of saying the Rosary, and attending daily Mass. God will send you new friends who love Him and who understand your new vocation.

Wisdom and peace are the fruits of carrying the Cross; raising a special needs child is your way of carrying the Cross. Try to offer it up for those mothers who are considering aborting a child like yours. It will make the suffering more meaningful. And remember to enjoy the unique gifts your special child offers to your family. Live in the joy of the moment, and don't be burdened by the future.

Remember that God gives the very best to those who leave the choice to Him. As He gave Jesus to the world on Christmas, He now gives you the vocation of special motherhood.

God loves you, and so do I.

Leticia

Part II

Special Mothers proclaim the Gospel of Life

KIDS Keep Infants with Down Syndrome meet with Rep Cathy McMorris Rodgers at the March for Life January 22, 2010

Chapter 36

When the war on our children began; the history of eugenic abortion

In this part of the book, I will take you through the tragic history of how our beautiful children became targets for destruction rather than fellow humans to be loved. How did America, the most prosperous nation on earth, whose laws are based on the natural law God has written into the hearts of mankind, become the place where over 90 percent of babies prenatally diagnosed with medical conditions such as Down syndrome are aborted? How did these precious children find themselves excluded from the right to "life, liberty, and the pursuit of happiness" inscribed in the Declaration of Independence?

It began in the 19th Century with a belief system called eugenics, which calls for the "purification" of mankind by positive and negative means. Positive eugenics involves selective breeding, which I did when I bred field champion Labrador Retrievers in my home. Negative eugenics involves the killing or sterilization of those whom society deems "unfit." Eugenics was imported from Europe, according to an article in *Contact Genetique Press Review* from the Jerome Lejeune Foundation in Paris:

"Eugenics first arose at the end of the 19th Century. The term was coined by Francis Galton, a cousin of Darwin, who saw it as the "science of improving heredity." For science historian André Pichot, it is "the desire to compensate for the demise of natural selection in human societies by establishing a kind of artificial selection." [1]

The eugenic movement rapidly had a major influence on legislation. In 1907, the state of Indiana authorized sterilization for particular types of criminals and sick people. Between the two world wars, its example was followed by certain countries: Switzerland (1928), Denmark (1929), Norway, Finland and Sweden (1935). The law of July 14, 1933, enacted by the Nazi regime and which imposed mandatory sterilization for people with 9 diseases considered to be hereditary or congenital, was accepted by almost the entire German medical corps, and was based on a Weimar Republic project drawn up in 1932.

"Eugenic laws therefore preceded the Nazi period, and survived it. In 1948, Japan authorized the government to impose sterilization for criminals 'with genetic predispositions to crime'. In Sweden, handicapped people were sterilized up until the 1980s." [2]

Tragically, eugenics took hold in the United States before World War II: African Americans, Latin Americans, and the mentally challenged were sterilized and used as subjects in scientific experiments by the government without their knowledge. In its 1926 Buck v. Bell decision, the U.S. Supreme Court decided that a woman who was pregnant out of wedlock should be forcibly sterilized. Writing for the majority opinion, Justice Oliver Wendell Holmes, Jr, stated:

"It would be strange if it could not call upon those who already sap the strength of the State for these lesser sacrifices, often not felt to be such by those concerned, in order to prevent our being swamped with incompetence. It is better for all the world, if instead of waiting to execute degenerate offspring for crime, or to let them starve for their imbecility, society can prevent those who are manifestly unfit from continuing their kind. The principle that sustains compulsory vaccination is broad enough to cover cutting the Fallopian tubes. Three generations of imbeciles are enough."[3]

Margaret Sanger, the founder of Planned Parenthood, began a eugenic contraceptive movement in 1916 in the immigrant tenements of New York City, aimed at poor mothers of so-called 'undesirable' races such as Latinos, African Americans and Jews. Like many eugenicists of the time, she was afraid that their children would be a burden on society. Here is an excerpt from a speech she gave, which appeared in her paper, *The Birth Control Review*, in 1926:

"It now remains for the U.S. government to set a sensible example to the world by offering a bonus or yearly pension to all obviously unfit parents who allow themselves to be sterilized by harmless and scientific means. In this way the moron and the diseased would have no posterity to inherit their unhappy condition. The number of the feeble-minded would decrease and a heavy burden would be lifted from the shoulders of the fit."[4]

Sanger went on to found Planned Parenthood, which has become the largest abortion provider in the United States, with branches around the world. Over 80 percent of Planned Parenthood facilities are in minority neighborhoods.

The eugenics movement was exposed in Ben Stein's film "Expelled: No Intelligence Allowed." I wrote about it in a piece for the website Catholic Exchange:

> "Stein followed the scientific community's lockstep loyalty to social Darwinism backwards in time, and ended up at the Nazi gas chambers, which first killed disabled people in the T4 Program. They were just practicing Darwinism by speeding up the process of natural selection, formerly called survival of the fittest, by eliminating "useless eaters." Society bought into this toxic mentality because it came from doctors and scientists.
>
> He followed their trail to Planned Parenthood founder Margaret Sanger, who was a dedicated eugenicist, working overtime to rid the world of people like my immigrant grandparents. While she was ostensibly offering women choice, secretly she was seeking to rid American society of the 'unfit': more Darwinism in action. We are still in the midst of the nightmare of Sanger's legacy: 52 million Americans have died of abortion, far surpassing the darkest dreams of Hitler and Stalin combined.
>
> If we continue to allow ourselves to be dominated by militantly atheistic scientists whose agenda blinds them to basic human dignity, we will find ourselves in a totalitarian state. The scientists who were interviewed in "Expelled" shamelessly admitted that they wish to destroy

the power religion holds on culture, and relegate it to an innocuous hobby, like knitting.

Political correctness will have replaced the Judeo-Christian belief in the dignity of man, the pinnacle and master of God's creation. We will find ourselves enslaved to a materialistic ideology. Our very right to exist will be determined by what the powerful consider a 'worthwhile contribution' to society, against our carbon footprint. Many of us — 'useless eaters' — may not make the cut. Terri Schiavo didn't."[5]

Again, the Jerome Lejeune Foundation, in their *Genethique Press Review,* points out that pre-natal diagnosis of disabled babies is a form of eugenics. "When screening for defects is systematic, organized and leads to the elimination of the sick children in most cases, this constitutes eugenics. Eugenics can be the result of a restrictive policy or be a consensual trend on the part of an entire society. Jean-François Mattei pointed out that although there is no "collective decision to eliminate sick or handicapped unborn children, in reality, the sum of all the individual decisions...amounts to the same thing."

"Stéphane Viville, of the Strasbourg University Hospital reproductive biology laboratory, admitted to being "disturbed" by the "systematic aspect" of defect detection. In his view, we are "verging" on eugenics because the social pressure is so great it leads women to have abortions almost systematically: "That's what's disturbing. There's no real free will." Perrine Malzac, a geneticist at La Timone Hospital in Marseilles, also noted: "The dominant discourse from doctors and the family means that, in practice, couples have little room to maneuver! Only those with very strong convictions are able to stand their ground."

Biologist Jacques Testart has always strongly protested against this selection of the "best embryo." This stance contrasts with society's general acceptance of diagnosis practices: no one seems to view them as violating the dignity of handicapped people."[6]

Many valiant bishops like Bishop Peter Elliot, head of Melbourne Australia's John Paul II Institute for Marriage and Family, have made statements alerting us to the warning signs of eugenics:

"The warped practice of eugenics is rising from its Nazi tomb in Australia. A seek-and-destroy policy kills little human beings in the womb because they are 'guilty' of Down syndrome, dwarfism or other imperfections.

"They are deemed to be unfit to live for they do not come up to the standard of the 'designer baby' and a healthy, sport-loving race. It is no surprise that euthanasia is being strongly promoted today. Nor should it be a surprise that this is the policy of a political and ideological force that puts more value on wattle and wombats than people.

"Resurgent aggressive secularism resorts to killing as it strives to engineer, direct and control not only society, but your life and mine."[7]

Even charitable organizations like the March of Dimes and Autism Speaks have spent thousands to research methods of pre-natal testing for Down syndrome and autism, which sounds beneficial at first. However, until these children can be treated in the womb, pre-natal testing will serve more as a search-and-destroy method of lowering birth defects statistics by destroying the less than perfect before they are born, rather than a method of improving the lives of families. In 1967, before abortion was legalized across America by Roe v Wade, and only permitted in states like New York, the American Medical Association issued a policy statement permitting abortion if there is "documented evidence that an infant may be born with an incapacity or physical deformity". Dr Henry Nadler of Children's Memorial Hospital in Boston, under March of Dimes funding, diagnosed the first unborn child with the condition, leading to the first abortion of a child with Down syndrome. This ironically was seen as a life-saving measure by the American public. Though not approving of abortion on demand for any reason, 55 percent approved of abortion for birth defects. Previously, a mother of a certain age (over 35) would be warned of her increased chances of carrying a child with Down syndrome, sometimes leading to abortion of 'normal' babies.[8]

Now it would be possible to select babies who would die, and let the healthy live. Eugenics via abortion began. This mentality is seen today as a new, non-invasive, maternal blood test named MaterniT21 is offering the promise of a 100 percent accurate pre-natal diagnosis of Down syndrome at the eighth week of pregnancy. It will be ready in early

2012. It is being hailed by the media as a life saving medical advance. Life saving for whom?

Medicine has claimed the power of life and death once owned by God alone, and families are burdened by discovery of prenatal testing and diagnosis with the choice to determine which children to have and which to abort. Many are pressured by doctors who advise abortion as matter of course and tell their patients horror stories about the difficulties of raising special needs children. They have told women that their marriages will fail, their older children will hate them and that their unborn child will never tie his shoes, learn to read, or have a happy life. These types of predictions are beyond medical prognosis and suggest a eugenic agenda.

Dr. Will Johnston, president of Canadian Physicians for Life, reacted to ACOG's pre-natal testing endorsement as another step toward eugenics. "The progress of eugenic abortion into the heart of our society is a classic example of "mission creep,'" Johnson said in an article posted on the group's Web site in February 2007. "In the 1960s, we were told that legal abortion would be a rare, tragic act in cases of exceptional hardship. In the '70s abortion began to be both decried and accepted as birth control. In the '80s respected geneticists pointed out that it was cheaper to hunt for and abort Down's babies than to raise them. By the '90s that observation had been widely put into action. Now we are refining and extending our eugenic vision, with new tests and abortion as our central tools."[9]

Tragically pre-natal diagnosis became possible through misguided use of the scientific innovations of two good Catholic doctors, Dr. Lejeune of France and Dr. Liley. It was Professor Liley, originally from New Zealand, who first invented the technique of prenatal diagnosis. He hoped that in this way one could detect and treat sick infants at an earlier stage of their development. Dr Lejeune, who discovered the cause of trisomy 21, was using every possible means to find out how to cure this condition. He, too, was convinced it ought to be cured very early, in utero. Thanks to amniocentesis and karyotyping ... the technology was in place for eliminating "undesirable specimens" before birth. Their discoveries were diverted from their original objective.[10]

Dr. Lejeune was heartbroken that his discovery was used to conduct search-and-destroy prenatal diagnosis and dedicated the rest his life to finding a cure for Down syndrome to overcome the catastrophic abortion rate. His work is continued by the Foundation Jerome Lejeune in Paris and the US.

Jean-Marie Le Méné, president of the *Fondation Jérôme Lejeune* says, "Children with Down syndrome, with their special physical features, pathologies, premature aging, mental retardation and dependence, seem in contradiction to all the demands for tyrannical happiness that our society aspires to." He points out that the French strategy for Down's syndrome screening is without equivalent in the world: €100 million are devoted to it each year, and 96 percent of children with Down's syndrome are aborted. "Women and families are made to feel guilty, unconcerned doctors may have to answer for the birth of an undesirable child and the state may be condemned for not offering the most effective screening system. Faced with this persecution, Le Méné calls on society to explore the real causes of the misfortune that does not lie in the Down's syndrome sufferers but in the disease itself."[11]

In the words of Dr. Lejeune, we are to "hate the disease, and love the patient: That is the practice of medicine." Loving people with Down syndrome may mean trying to find treatment for trisomy 21 in order to lessen mothers' fears of carrying their children to term. Dr Lejeune said, "The task is immense, but so is hope." He insisted that, "It will take much less intellectual effort than sending a man to the Moon."[12]

His philosophy lives on in the Foundation begun by his family. "The same position is defended by Dr. Henri Bléhaut, from the Fondation Jérôme Lejeune, who states that the response to the fear of future mothers to have a disabled child is above all medical: "We have to find a treatment against intellectual deficiency, particularly the one involved in Down syndrome." In the light of the incredible progress made by medicine in recent years, he says that it is possible to find a treatment for Down syndrome. "Of course, after much work, research, time and obstacles overcome, but it is possible. Why would it be an exceptional disease, inaccessible to therapy?" The Jérôme Lejeune Foundation finances and participates in a number of projects in this area. Some are trying to intervene directly on the genotype, i.e. on the genes of chromosome 21 such as CBS (CiBleS21 project) or DYRK1A. Others are working on patients' phenotype, i.e. on the abnormal functioning of the central nervous system provoked by Down syndrome."[13]

It is an uphill climb. Once abortion was accepted by the international medical community as a solution to the 'problem' of trisomy 21, research was nearly abandoned, and it was considered good practice for health care workers to advise abortion as a 'cure.' Only the perseverance of Dr. Lejeune kept hope alive that better days were coming for those who have extra chromosomes.

That is why this book is so timely; as health care becomes nationalized in the United States, soon the decision to abort these precious gifts from God could become policy, rather than a choice. We know this from our friends in Europe and Canada, where socialized medicine leads to cost-cutting measures and denial of care to those whose lives are considered too costly to maintain. The Canadian Pediatric Society has recently taken a position that newborn babies with defects like Down syndrome may be denied hydration and food at the wishes of their parents.[14] This is a natural extension of abortion throughout all nine months of pregnancy. It won't be just newborns who are denied care. The case of baby Joseph Maarachli, who was refused a tracheotomy and ventilator in a London, Ontario hospital, stands as an example. Fr. Frank Pavone of Priests for Life financed a private jet to transfer Joseph to a Catholic hospital in St Louis, MO, where he received the tracheotomy that extended his life. He was baptized and sent home to be surrounded by his family, not sentenced to die by medical order in a hospital. At the time I write this, Baby Joseph recently went home to God, at home, in the arms of his family. How much longer will the United States continue to be the safe haven for babies such as Joseph? If not here, then where can such families turn for help when the state decides to withhold basic medical treatment from their disabled child?

The national health care system of New Zealand has recently recommended universal testing for Down syndrome. What do you think will happen to parents whose child is prenatally diagnosed with Down syndrome? Will they be pressured to abort their child by a panel of advisors, which Sarah Palin correctly called "death panels"? Where will they go if they want to fight for their child's life? What will happen to their child when her parents are no longer alive to fight for her? Novelist Michelle Buckman wrote a chilling novel called, *The Death Panels*, based on such a national health care system. It reads like Aldous Huxley's *Brave New World*. We may be on the brink of enforced eugenics.

On what basis do I make this prediction? Medical 'ethicists' have already begun to establish means to quantitatively measure the relative worth of a human life, to determine the cost effectiveness of treating a patient's medical condition. An equation has been developed—QALY (quality of adjusted life years)—which calculates the worth of a human being's quality of life. This enables the medical establishment to compare the value of performing a medical procedure on one person relative to another, a form of triage, similar to what is done in hospital emergency rooms when deciding whose condition to treat first. QALY uses a formula which combines subjective assessments of whether the quality of a person's life merits certain medical treatment. It is a cost-cutting measure which reduces people to numbers. It's based on interviews with people who have debilitating conditions and average life expectancy of people with such conditions. The patient will be assigned a number, based on the formula, and advocates would have people use these QALY numbers to line up in numerical order for treatment such as heart surgery.[15]

Here is the chilling opinion of Princeton Bioethicist Peter Singer, who is widely respected in academic circles, as quoted by the Institute for Social Ecology:

> "Down syndrome, once again a genetically based condition gets the most attention in Singer's recent work. His 1994 book, *Rethinking Life & Death*, which seeks to articulate 'a social ethic where some human lives are valued and others are not' (p. 112), recapitulates the arguments in favor of selective infanticide outlined above. There he endorses the view that 'it is ethical that a child suffering from Down syndrome...should not survive' (p. 123) because 'the quality of life of someone with Down syndrome [is] below the standard at which medical treatment to sustain the life of an infant becomes obligatory.' (p. 111) In Singer's terms, 'treatment to sustain life' doesn't refer merely to surgical intervention, but to simple feeding as well. This 'quality of life' reasoning is sometimes cast

in more colorful terms. In *Should the Baby Live?* Singer quotes, entirely approvingly, the grandmother of a child with Down syndrome: 'Had the poor little mongol been allowed to die, as he so easily could, my daughter might have had one or two healthy children in his place.' (p. 66) Singer goes on to suggest lethal injection 'in the case of a Down syndrome baby with no other defect.' (p. 73) [15]

But how can we measure another human being's quality of life? Over 20 years ago, the average life span of a person with Down syndrome was 25 years. Now it is 50 years and growing. Why? Was there some marvelous research done which accounts for the doubling of their life expectancy? No. Since the 1980s, doctors have decided that babies with Down syndrome were "worth" the effort to repair their hearts. Before this, life-saving surgery was possible, but "simply not done" on patients with Down syndrome. It was a matter of judgment that people with Down syndrome had a sufficient quality of life to merit the surgery. What made the difference? Families of such patients, and increasingly the patients themselves have become advocates. Advocates for equal access to education and advocates for access to life-saving treatments and life-extending research dollars. Thanks to parents contacting their legislators, the Congressional Down Syndrome Caucus was formed by Rep. Cathy McMorris Rodgers (WA-R), whose young son, Cole, has Down syndrome. This caucus has advocated for the National Institute of Health to develop their first research plan for Down syndrome, and the NIH is considering increasing funding such promising research as I describe in my article in the National Catholic Register, "Down Not Out" (see Appendix II).

Much more needs to be done until society regards our children as persons with an inalienable right to life, and not as a disability or medical condition. An example is when we say, "the Down's child." We must correct this and say, "No, she is a child who has Down syndrome." As always, when there is an assault on the dignity of human life, Holy Mother Church responds. During his November 2010 trip to Spain, Pope Benedict XVI spent time blessing the Nedu home for the disabled in Barcelona, and spoke the following words to resounding applause,

"It is clear that, for the Christian, every man and woman is a true sanctuary of God, and should be treated with the highest respect and affection, above all, when they are in need. It is indispensable that new technological developments in the field of medicine never be to the detriment of human respect or dignity, so that those who suffer physical illness or handicaps can always receive that love and attention required to make them feel fully valued as persons in their concrete needs. I assure you that you have a special place in the Pope's heart. I pray for you every day and ask you to help me by means of your prayers, so that I may faithfully fulfill the mission entrusted to me by Christ".[16]

Will Catholic parents of special needs children stand in solidarity with the Holy Father, and oppose the culture of death? Will we raise our voices in the public square, insisting that our children have intrinsic worth given to them by God, demanding that they be allowed to live?

END NOTES

1 . Eibl, Florence, Pierre-Olivier Arduin, Jean-Marie Le Méné, and Dr. Henri Bléhaut.
"Press Review from 04th to 08th of October 2010."*Genethique.org : Revue De Presse Et Dossiers En Bioéthique. Actualités Clonage, Avortement, Fécondation in Vitro, Fin De Vie, Euthanasie, Cellules Souches, Embryons.* Oct. 2010. Web. <http://www.genethique.org/En/press/press/2010/October/04_08.html>.

2. Ibid

3. Buck v. Bell. Supreme Court. 1927. Print.

4. "BlackGenocide.org | The Truth About Margaret Sanger." *BlackGenocide.org | L.E.A.R.N. Northeast.* 20 Jan. 1992. Web. <http://www.blackgenocide.org/sanger.html>.

Leticia Velasquez

5. Velasquez, Leticia. "The History of Eugenics Is in Expelled | Catholic Exchange." *Catholic Exchange - Daily Catholic News, Catholic Articles, Catholic Apologetics, Catholic Content, Catholic Information.* 9 May 2008. Web. <http://catholicexchange.com/2008/05/09/112398/>.

6. Eibl, Florence, Pierre-Olivier Arduin, Jean-Marie Le Méné, and Dr. Henri Bléhaut.
Press Review from 04th to 08th of October 2010."*Genethique.org : Revue De Presse Et Dossiers En Bioéthique. Actualités Clonage, Avortement, Fécondation in Vitro, Fin De Vie, Euthanasie, Cellules Souches, Embryons.* Oct. 2010. Web. <http://www.genethique.org/En/press/press/2010/October/04_08.html>.

7. Livingston, Tess. "Eugenics 'rising from Nazi Tomb' in Victoria, Claims Bishop Peter Elliott | News.com.au." *News.com.au | News Online from Australia & the World | NewsComAu.* 5 Nov. 2010. Web. <http://www.news.com.au/national/eugenics-rising-from-nazi-tomb-in-victorian-claims-bishop-peter-elliott/story-e6frfkvr-1225948099647>.

8. Engel, Randy. *A March of Dimes Primer: The A-Z of Genetic Killing.* Michael Fund. Print.

9. Starr, Penny. "'Eugenic Abortion': With Pre-Natal Testing, 9 in 10 Down Syndrome Babies Aborted | CNSnews.com." *CNS News | CNSnews.com.* 13 Oct. 2008. Web. <http://www.cnsnews.com/news/article/37421>.

10. Lejeune, Clara. *Life Is a Blessing.* San Francisco: Ignatius. 45-46. Print.

11. Eibl, Florence, Pierre-Olivier Arduin, Jean-Marie Le Méné, and Dr. Henri Bléhaut.
Press Review from 04th to 08th of October 2010."*Genethique.org : Revue De Presse Et Dossiers En Bioéthique. Actualités Clonage, Avortement, Fécondation in Vitro, Fin De Vie, Euthanasie, Cellules Souches, Embryons.* Oct. 2010. Web. <http://www.genethique.org/En/press/press/2010/October/04_08.html>.

12. Lejeune, Jerome. "*21 Thoughts by Jerome Lejeune*" Lejeune USA. Print.

13. Eibl, Florence, Pierre-Olivier Arduin, Jean-Marie Le Méné, and Dr. Henri Bléhaut.
Press Review from 04th to 08th of October 2010."*Genethique.org : Revue De Presse Et Dossiers En Bioéthique. Actualités Clonage, Avortement, Fécondation in Vitro, Fin De Vie,*

Euthanasie, Cellules Souches, Embryons. Oct. 2010. Web. <http://www.genethique. org/En/press/press/2010/October/04_08.html>.

14. Schadenberg, Alex. "Canadian Paediatric Approves the Dehydration of Infants Who May Not Be Otherwise Dying." *LifeSiteNews.com.* 4 Apr. 2011. Web. <http:// www.lifesitenews.com/news/canadian-paediatric-approves-the-dehydration-of-infants-who-may-not-be-othe/>.

15, Phillips, Ceri, and Guy Thompson. "QALY." *Bandolier "Evidence-based Thinking about Health Care"* Apr. 2009. Web. <http://www.medicine.ox.ac.uk/bandolier/booth/glossary/QALY.html>.

16. Staudenmaier, Peter. "Peter Singer and Eugenics | Institute for Social Ecology." *The Institute for Social Ecology.* 1 Jan. 2005. Web. <http://www.social-ecology.org/2005/01/peter-singer-and-eugenics/>.

16. "Rome Reports." *Pope Visits Center for the Disabled.* Rome, Italy, 7 Nov. 2010. Television.

Eileen Haupt and Leticia Velasquez, co-founders of KIDS with Colleen
Carroll Campbell on the set of the EWTN show 'Faith and Culture

Chapter 37

Special Mothers Respond

It was the Feast of the Sorrowful Mother, a brilliantly sunny fall morning
of September 15, 2009. In my trembling hand, I was holding a prepared
speech from the International Down Syndrome Coalition for Life and
an 8x10 photo of Christina. Television cameras were arranged in rows
on "the Triangle" on Capitol Hill, as I nervously took my place among
the dozen parents of special needs children. I was there with Kristen
Hawkins, director of Health Care for Gunner, Rep. Trent Franks (AZ-R),
and Rep. Cathy McMorris Rodgers (WA-R) to give a press conference
warning Americans that under the health care proposal being considered
by Congress, our special needs children would not be covered. We feared
that their lives were threatened, as well as those children yet unborn with
the same conditions. Mary Kellett and Eileen Benthal as well as other

parents from the US and Canada were there, to bear witness to the value of our children's lives to our families and to our nation. Here is the text of my speech,

> "My name is Leticia Velasquez and I am the mother of Christina, who is seven. She attends first grade in a public school in Connecticut. Christina has Down syndrome.
>
> "I represent the International Down Syndrome Coalition for Life. The IDSC for Life has two major concerns with the current bill. The first concern is for the child who is in the womb, and is diagnosed with Down syndrome. Currently, the termination rate for children who are diagnosed in utero is reported to be near 90 percent in America. The International Down Syndrome Coalition for Life is concerned that the current health care bill will encourage families to abort the life of a child who happens to have Down syndrome, in the name of cost effectiveness.
>
> "Will there be a panel that will decide that the price savings of terminating the pregnancy outweighs the dignity and value of the life of a child? Will it then become a patriotic responsibility to end a life that others deem less than perfect? Will there be measures written into the reform that protest the life of a child diagnosed prenatally with special needs?
>
> "Since the goal of the healthcare reform bill as it is written is to help save the nation money, the IDSC for Life believes these are vital concerns which must be addressed.
>
> "Our second major concern pertains to the individuals with Down syndrome who have been born. Currently, these people are given therapies and life-saving surgeries

to help enhance the quality of their lives. Under HR 3200, can we be sure that this will continue? Will their medical concerns be treated equally with individuals who do not have Down syndrome? The IDSC for life is very concerned that our children, grandchildren, sisters, brothers and friends will not be given equal access to health care, because of their diagnosis. We believe that each individual deserves medical care that is needed to ensure that they can live full and happy lives. We cannot help but wonder if this health care reform act will actually lower the quality of care that our loved ones require.

"The IDSC for Life would like to see provisions in any health care reform bill which will ensure the protection of the lives of individuals with disabilities. We believe those provisions must be written into any health care reform to protect those in the womb, and those who are already born."

This event was carried all over the world by the Associated Press, and even though we did not stop that legislation from becoming law, we are still fighting to overturn that law. We have proven that the power of mothers fighting for their children is a force with which to be reckoned. We spread out on Capitol Hill, speaking personally with our elected representatives to voice our concerns, to no avail. Obamacare was passed by deceit, by the president assuring us that it would not lead to rationing of care or to taxpayer funding of abortions. Now 26 states have joined a lawsuit to challenge the constitutionality of Obamacare, and those who supported it were soundly defeated in the midterm elections of 2010.

Another powerful movement was the reaction of parents of children with Down syndrome in January 2007, when, in the *New Practice Bulletin*, the American College of Obstetricians and Gynecologists recommended that *all* pregnant women, regardless of age, be offered testing for trisomy 21. A huge grassroots movement began, which *New York Times* reporter Amy Harmon described in her piece "The DNA Age: New Prenatal Test

Puts Down syndrome in Hard Focus" May 6, 2007. She won a Pulitzer Prize for "The DNA Age" series.[1]

The momentum built. Parents of children with trisomy 21 began blogs, started petitions, made YouTube videos and used social media to call attention to the deliberate singling out of their children for pre-natal 'search-and-destroy' missions. Our activism bore fruit when, in September 2008, the Prenatally Diagnosed Conditions Awareness Act, S 1810, was passed, thanks to the across-the-aisle sponsorship of former senators Edward Kennedy (D-MA) and Samuel Brownback (R-KS). President George Bush signed it into law on October 10, 2008. The law provides for collection and dissemination of accurate information on Down syndrome and other conditions diagnosed in utero. It also calls for the establishment of a telephone hotline, support networks and educational programs for expectant parents and healthcare providers. Finally, it sets up a national registry of people interested in adopting children with genetic conditions. Rep. Cathy McMorris Rodgers (WA-R) is working with the House Appropriations Committee to ensure funding for these programs.

Shortly after the legislation passed, The University of South Carolina's Genetic Counseling Program and the University's Center for Disability Resources hosted a meeting with the American College of Medical Genetics, the National Society of Genetic Counselors, the National Down Syndrome Society, the National Down Syndrome Congress and the American College of Obstetrics and Gynecology. At this meeting, they wrote a document titled "Toward Concurrence," in which they stated how important it is to get positive information about the productive and happy lives of most people with Down syndrome out to the general public. I commend their efforts in programs such as NDSS's "My Great Story," where self advocates speak about their accomplishments. These programs give hope to those of us raising our children and worrying about the future.

Tragically, the writers of this document made a critical mistake in asserting in no uncertain terms that the National Down Syndrome Society and the National Down Syndrome Congress are *not* pro-life organizations. They go on to deny that the purpose of prenatal testing is to 'search and destroy' unborn children with disabilities, and deny the

92 percent abortion rate, stating, "No current, comprehensive estimate of the number of pregnancy terminations following prenatal diagnosis exists."[2] This statistic was established by the research of Dr. Brian Skotko in his paper titled, "With new prenatal testing, will babies with Down syndrome slowly disappear?" which appeared in the *Archives of Disease in Childhood*.[3] These organizations deny the overwhelming evidence in Dr. Skotko's research that women often feel pressured by their obstetricians to abort their babies with Down syndrome.

I have spoken to Down syndrome research organizations in the United States and abroad, and only the Jerome Lejeune Foundation will state publicly that they are pro-life, out of fear that they will lose research money. The Jerome Lejeune Foundation does not allow its researchers to use embryonic stem cells and verifies this by twice yearly inspections. Two more organizations which are openly pro-life have risen to fill the need for advocates for our children from conception to natural death: my own KIDS Keep Infants with Down Syndrome and our sister organization, International Down Syndrome Coalition for Life, founded by contributor Diane Grover. Here is how Grover describes her journey.

> "I am the mother of five beautiful children whom I have home schooled since my oldest was in second grade," says Grover. "He is now in college. My husband and I have always believed that all life is precious from conception to natural death. However, when our daughter was born, we became aware of the percentage of children that were being aborted when their parents found out they were expecting a child with Down syndrome. This absolutely broke our hearts.
>
> New things would happen every day that increased our awareness of this sad statistic. We had an encounter while we were getting ice cream one day. A mother approached us with tears in her eyes, and asked if she could hold our daughter. She then proceeded to tell us that she had 'bought the lie.' She said she believed the doctors when they told her that she would not be able to handle a child

who happened to have Down syndrome. She terminated her pregnancy. A couple of years later, her best friend had a little girl with Down syndrome. She explained to us how she grieved her loss every time she saw a child with Down syndrome. She told us her baby was a boy, and that she missed him very much.

After this encounter, we realized that we needed to find a way for parents to connect to healing. We wanted also to create a way for those who had children who happened to have Down syndrome, and are pro life, to be able to express those views. The larger Down syndrome organizations have a position to not have a position, so we wanted to create an organization where parents could come together to support each other and to advocate for the life of individuals in the womb and in the room. This is when and how the International Down Syndrome Coalition for Life (IDSC for Life) was born. We came together with many other families. This has allowed us to share with others that we believe that ALL life is precious, including those who happen to have Down syndrome.

We have been able to connect families who have terminated their pregnancies to Lumina (an organization affiliated with the Sisters of Life, which offers retreats for those who aborted a child with special needs), for healing and hope. Our hearts go out to all of the mothers who, like that mother, believed it would be too hard. All of us were scared at one time, and we understand their fears. Our hope is that they can find healing and hope through our efforts. We are just an average family that saw a need and acted on that need. I am busy with my own sweet family, so I have had to weave this between all of our activities. But it has been a blessing to work with so many wonderful families, and help to advocate in the room and in the womb. All of our little efforts have come together to create a wonderful organization. The IDSC continues to grow and be a voice for the many families out there that believe all life is precious!"

Those of you whose children have other diagnoses are similarly targeted. A recent article on the spending of the charity Autism Speaks reveals not only gross overspending on the salaries of the directors, but a focus on research on the genetic markers of autism. These markers may soon lead to pre-natal diagnosis for autism and other conditions. Soon, children with autism will face similar patterns of extinction as those we face in the Down syndrome community. Currently there are large amounts of money put into research to treat autism, but if the numbers of children with autism are decimated by eugenic abortion, the influence of the autism community will diminish in the same manner as that of the Down syndrome community, according to Dana Commandatore of Big Government blog,

"Instead of funding services for families and individuals, Autism Speaks' operating budget goes primarily towards research on the cause of autism, much of it devoted to finding particular genes with an eye to developing a prenatal test. As families of children with Down syndrome are aware, the existence of prenatal testing for autism means a vast increase in the eugenic abortion of children with autism before they are born."[4]

If we spend our precious research dollars on search-and-destroy technology for specific genetic conditions, we squander unparalleled research opportunities, not only to alleviate suffering by those with disabilities, but by the general public as well. The research for treatment of physical defects as well as learning and memory problems for people with Down syndrome has never been brighter. Dr. William Mobley told a packed audience at world renowned genetic research facility Cold Spring Harbor Laboratory in 2009, that within a decade a drug may be available to normalize the cognition and memory of people with Down syndrome (See my article "Down Not Out" for more discussion of research on Down syndrome in Appendix II). Dr Mobley said, in a recent article, "I've never been more optimistic about the future of Down syndrome research than I am right now. My colleagues and I are energized as never before to make a positive contribution to the well being of people with Down syndrome and their families".[5] Dr. Roger Reeves, a trisomy 21 researcher at Johns Hopkins University, while describing his research, said that the fact that people with Down syndrome rarely suffer from cancerous tumors may unlock the secret to cancer treatment for the rest of us, so his research received National Cancer Institute funding. New studies offer hope that the unique genetic structure of Down syndrome may also offer clues to the treatment of Alzheimer's disease. Dr. Reeves is also optimistic about recent research advances and said "We really are in the early stages of a revolution in understanding the basis for many of the features which occur in Down syndrome"[6]

We owe this promising research to the scientific legacy of a devout Catholic. Dr. Jerome Lejeune, the French geneticist who, in 1958, discovered trisomy 21, the cause of Down syndrome, and dedicated his life to finding a cure because, as he told his assistant, Dr. Marie Peeters-Ney, "As Catholic doctors we have an obligation to research a cure for Down syndrome. If we don't there won't be any people with Down syndrome left." He said, "Pre-natal diagnosis of Down syndrome for purposes of abortion is a desperate mockery of science".[7] His efforts to save our children and to bear witness to the truth that life begins at conception were rejected by the world, which failed to recognize his landmark discovery of trisomy 21 for the Nobel Prize. Dr. Lejeune's scientific genius and devotion to upholding the sanctity of human life were not missed by the late Pope John Paul II, however. The two great men were friends; Pope John Paul II appointed Dr. Lejeune to the Pontifical Academy of Science, and named him founding director of the Pontifical Academy of Life, as he lay on his deathbed from cancer in 1994. "I am dying while on special duty," the good doctor exclaimed. But, as we know, saints like St Therese of Lisieux only continue their good works from Heaven. On June 28, 2007, the cause for canonization of Dr. Jerome Lejeune was opened. His reputation for personal sanctity and love for those whom the world rejected make him a natural patron of those with Down syndrome and others whose genetic conditions threaten their lives.

Our Lord said, "Much will be required of the person entrusted with much." Luke 12:48 NABRE. In the first section of *A Special Mother is Born*, my friends and I shared with you how the blessings of our Catholic faith have enabled us to do little things with great love for our precious children, whom the world deems incomplete or broken. We have learned to count it all joy when we are facing life-threatening challenges, thanks to God changing our hearts through the blessings of our children. But sharing our stories with you is only the beginning. Now is the time to stand our lamps on top of the bushel basket, and let our children's lights shine from our homes to the world, penetrating the darkness of the culture of death and transforming society. Pope Benedict, in his homily in Nazareth on May 14, 2009, said,

> "In the family, each person, whether the smallest child or the oldest relative, is valued for him or herself, and not seen simply as a means to some other end. Here we begin to glimpse something of the essential role of the family as the first building-block of a well-ordered and welcoming society."[8]

Dr. Lejeune said, "In modern democracies, which no longer refer to a higher moral law, upright citizens have an innate duty to aspire to laws that reflect what they believe to be best for society: that is the only duty incumbent upon them, and the only freedom they still possess."[9]

How should you go about the daunting task of building a culture of life? I suggest that you begin on your knees before the Blessed Sacrament. Ask Our Lord to show you what He wants you to do with the talents He has given you.

Then, re-read these stories and see how our special mothers and fathers changed the lives of those around them. Some, like Eileen Benthal, were such powerful witnesses by their unwavering faith, dedicated love, and devout prayer at their child's bedside, that they changed their doctors' lives. Johanna Benthal's neurosurgeon converted to Catholicism and became a speaker on eugenics and the dignity of human life.

Some, like Diane Grover, Mary Kellett, Gretchen Peters, Eileen Haupt and I, began organizations to help expectant mothers in crisis over pre-natal diagnoses, or call attention to the 92 percent abortion rate of our children. Others like Barbara Curtis, Lisa Barker, Kate Basi, Margaret Mary Meyers, Therese Royals, Christina Bogdan, Kimberlee Kallan-Kaden, Helen Dilworth, Dr Gerard Nadal, Mary Ellen Barrett, and Melissa Wiley, wrote moving stories in their blogs about the gifts their children brought to their families. Barbara Curtis' talented daughter Maddy was featured as a contestant on *American Idol*, which led to her widely seen TV biography describing her family with Jon and her adopted brothers with Down syndrome. Former Senator Rick Santorum shares his pro-life views in the Ethics and Public Policy Center, *The Philadelphia Inquirer*, and on the campaign trail as he seeks the Republican nomination for the presidency. Dr. Judy Mascolo and nurses Jane O'Friel, Jane McGuire, and Nancy Valko incorporate their love for special needs children into their health care practices. Dr. Mascolo speaks on pro-life medical practice across Connecticut. Nancy Valko has appeared on the EWTN show "Faith and Culture" to discuss issues in health care, is a pro-life speaker, and Spokesman for the board of the National Association of Pro-life Nurses. Jane O'Friel founded "Respecting Inclusive Educational Needs," an inclusive Catholic education program. Allison Gringas is hoping to publish her two books while running an apostolate of Catholic evangelization called "Reconciled to You." There is no limit on the ways in which Catholic special needs mothers are living out their call to be salt and light to the world.

Thanks to my conviction that the tragic abortion rate of children with Down syndrome would be reduced if the world knew how beautiful Christina is and how much she enriches my family, I began the writing career I had put off for over 20 years. I now work full time out of my home writing and speaking about this and related topics. We have all accomplished these feats thanks to the Spirit of God, to whom we gave a simple "yes." Is He calling you in a similar manner? If He is, contact me at: marysjoys@yahoo.com and we will find a way to work together using your gifts to help the world appreciate the unique beauty we see in our children.

What if your child's condition is such that you can barely handle his daily care? Please don't discount the immeasurable value of the most powerful force on earth: humility united with suffering. This book was published because Rebecca Harrison-Barker's suffering was offered for the success of this book Her mother could do more than care for her with patient love, praying for her as she journeyed home to God. Lisa offered her suffering, united with that of her daughter, for the publication of this book. All my efforts pale beside the breathtaking power of a suffering mother's prayer offered in unity with the Cross of Christ.

There are mothers who were unable to take time to share here, but offered to pray for us as we wrote our stories. It was the profound suffering of Christ and His Mother Mary which brought about the greatest event of human history: the salvation of mankind. Each special mother is called to be part of this response to the culture of death which asks the question, "Who cares about the life of this child with special needs?" with a resounding "God does and so do we!"

During World Youth Day in Madrid, the Holy Father met with disabled students and said,

> "Jesus and, in his footsteps, his Sorrowful Mother and the saints, are witnesses who show us how to experience the tragedy of suffering for our own good and for the salvation of the world. These witnesses speak to us, first and foremost, of the dignity of all human life, created in the image of God".[9]

The Holy Father went on to say that God wanted to share with us his particular love for those who are suffering in His Passion,

> "because the Son of God wanted freely to embrace suffering and death, we are also capable of seeing God's image in the face of those who suffer. This preferential love of the Lord for the suffering helps us to see others more clearly and to give them, above and beyond their material demands, the look of love which they need" [10]

Only by knowing Christ in a personal manner, the pontiff counseled, can we see beyond the ravages of disease on the body, and see the beauty of Christ in the soul of those who need our compassion. And, in helping them, we find our hearts healed and opened to God. In the end it is we who are indebted to them for what they have given to us.

> "In a mysterious yet real way, their presence awakens in our often hardened hearts a tenderness which opens us to salvation. The lives of these young people surely touch human hearts and for that reason we are grateful to the Lord for having known them."[11]

Our children are not only our means of achieving eternal sanctity; they are God's gift to a hurting world.

END NOTES

1. Harmon, Amy. "The DNA Age: New Prenatal Test Puts Down Syndrome in Hard Focus." *New York Times*. 9 May 2007. Web. <http://www.nytimes.com/2007/05/09/us/09down.html>.

2. Edwards, Janice G., and Richard R. Ferrante. *Toward Concurrence: Understanding Prenatal Screening and Diagnosis of Down Syndrome from the Health Professional and Advocacy Community Perspectives.* New York, NY: National Down Syndrome Society, 2009. Print.

3. Skotko, Brian. "With New Prenatal Testing, Will Babies with Down Syndrome Slowly Disappear?"*BrianSkotko.com*. 22 Oct. 2009. Web. <http://www.brianskotko.com/index.php?option=com_content&task=blogcategory&id=4&Itemid=7>.

4. Commandatore, Dana. "» Sebelius Appoints the $600,000 Woman Federal Autism Panel - Big Government." *Big Government*. 4 May 2010. Web. <http://biggovernment.com/dcommandatore/2010/05/04/sibelius-appoints-the-600000-woman-to-federal-autism-panel/>.

5. Nugent, Tom. "Climbing the "Mountain of Hope"" *Nebraska Magazine* 30 Sept. 2010: 30-36.*Http://issuu.com/nebraskaalumni/docs/nebmagfall2010*. Web.

6. Down Syndrome Research and Treatment Foundation website < http://www.dsrtf.org/>

7. Lejeune, Jerome. *"21 Thoughts by Jerome Lejeune"* Lejeune USA

8. Baklinski, Thaddeus M. "Pope: The Family Is Essential For Building A Civilization Of Love."*LifeSiteNews.com*. 19 May 2009. Web. <http://www.lifesitenews.com/news/archive/ldn/2009/may/09051902>.

9. "Pope's Address to Youth with Illnesses and Disabilities", *ZENIT.org*, 2011-08-Web<http://www.zenit.org/article-33244?l=english>

10. Ibid

11. Ibid

Appendix I

Pro-life Resources for Special Needs Parenting

WEBSITES

PRENATAL PARTNERS FOR LIFE

Prenatal Partners for Life is a group of concerned parents (most of whom have or had a special needs child) medical professionals, legal professionals and clergy whose aim is to support, inform and encourage expectant or new parents. We offer support by connecting parents facing an adverse diagnosis with other parents who have had the same diagnosis. We have many resources such as adoption agencies with clients waiting to adopt and love a special needs child should a parent feel they could not care for them.

We believe each child is a special gift from God

www.prenatalpartnersforlife.com

BE NOT AFRAID

Benotafraid.net is an online outreach to parents who have received a poor or difficult prenatal diagnosis. The family stories, articles, and links within this site are presented as a resource for those who may have been asked to choose between terminating a pregnancy or continuing on despite the diagnosis. The benotafraid.net families faced the same decision and chose not to terminate. By sharing our experiences, we hope to offer encouragement to those who may be afraid to continue on.

www.benotafraid.net

INTERNATIONAL DOWN SYNDROME COALITION FOR LIFE

Dedicated to promoting the dignity and respect for all individuals with Down syndrome, from conception and throughout life. We are a coalition that has worldwide representation. Our mission is to celebrate and enhance the lives of individuals with Down syndrome, as well as to ensure fair and accurate representation in the case of prenatal diagnosis. IDSC For Life will accomplish this mission by educating medical staff and families with a prenatal diagnosis as well as offering current and up to date information.

www.IDSC.com

PREEMIE PRINTS

Preemie Prints is a 501(c)3 non profit organization dedicated to sharing hope with families experiencing the difficulties of a premature birth through information, photography, gift bags, support, and prayer. Preemie prints goes to the hospital or your home to take a free photo of your baby, has online prayer support, and is forming a local support group in Columbus, Ohio.

www.preemieprints.blogspot.com

THE APOSTOLATE OF HANNAH'S TEARS

We offer prayer support and comfort to the brokenhearted who suffer the pains of infertility at any stage of life, difficult pregnancy, miscarriage, stillbirth, the loss of a child and the adoption process. This apostolate intercedes for Catholic doctors, nurses, and their supportive personnel. We also serve as a vehicle of education in the proper channels of Catholic fertility practices as well as offering information resources to those seeking adoption and fertility care.

Contact person Therese Garcia
www.theapostolateofhannahstears

BACK IN HIS ARMS AGAIN

During a time of grief and pain, Back in His Arms Again is a ministry of collaborative resources providing care, compassion, faith, guidance, and support to those experiencing loss as well as those providing care.

www.backinhisarmsagain.com

KIDS (KEEP INFANTS WITH DOWN SYNDROME)

Organization of pro-life parents of children with Down syndrome who want to raise awareness of the 92% abortion rate of babies with Down syndrome. We attend the March for Life in Washington and state pro-life marches, use all types of media, and meet with Congressmen.

Contact people: Eileen Haupt and Leticia Velasquez
www.KeepInfantswithDownSyndrome.blogspot.com

PKS KIDS
A non-profit organization formed to provide education, awareness and support for those touched with Pallister-Killian syndrome
www.pkskids.com or email us at info@pkskids.net

DVDS/CD'S

MR. BLUE SKY
Love story between a young woman with Down syndrome and a typical man who fall in love and marry despite obstacles. Available on DVD.
www.mrblueskymovie.com

SIGNING TIME
A popular series of videos which teach American Sign Language to children. This series comes highly recommended by parents of children with Down syndrome.
www.Signingtime.com

THE MEMORY KEEPER'S DAUGHTER
Lifetime films
(see the book by the same name)

MONICA AND DAVID
Tribeca Film Festival Award Wining documentary about a married couple with Down syndrome
www.monicaanddavid.com

BOOKS

All are available on Amazon and Barnes and Noble websites

SOMETIMES MIRACLES HIDE: STIRRING LETTERS FROM THOSE WHO DISCOVERED GOD'S BLESSINGS IN A SPECIAL CHILD

Award winning song by Christian Singer Bruce Carroll with book of letters from parents of special needs children inspired by the song. Has CD with the song in the book.

THE DEATH PANELS
Michelle Buckman

Novel which predicts the terrifying society where government controls all life and death health care decisions and a baby boy with Down syndrome who is the victim of death panels.

MAKING A CASE FOR LIFE: A NEW DEFINITION OF PERFECTION
Stephanie Winick, RN.

Registered nurse Stephanie Winick makes a compelling case for the contributions individuals with Down syndrome make to society and argues against the 92% abortion rate of those who are pre-natally diagnosed.

THE MEMORY KEEPER'S DAUGHTER
By Kim Edwards

Best selling novel about a doctor who delivers his own twins in the 1960's, a boy and a girl with Down syndrome. His wife is told the girl has died and the doctor gives her to his nurse to institutionalize, but she can't make herself and decides to raise her as her own.

ROADMAP TO HOLLAND
Jennifer Graf Groneburg

A mother with premature twin boys, one of whom has Down syndrome, shares the intimate details of their early lives and her inner journey towards peace.

GIFTS: MOTHERS REFLECT ON HOW CHILDREN WITH DOWN SYNDROME ENRICH THEIR LIVES
Kathryn Lynard Soper

Sixty three mothers of different faith backgrounds share their birth stories and how their child with Down syndrome became a beloved member of their family.

COMMON THREADS: CELEBRATING LIFE WITH DOWN SYNDROME
Dr Brian G Skotko and Cynthia S. Kidde
Coffee table book celebrating the lives of those with Down syndrome.

ANGEL UNAWARE; A TOUCHING STORY OF LOVE AND LOSS
Dale Evans Rogers
TV personality and wife of Roy Rogers bestselling 1953 book which tells the story of their daughter Robin Elizabeth born in 1950 with Down syndrome.

ANOTHER SEASON: A COACH'S STORY OF RAISING AN EXCEPTIONAL SON
Gene Stallings and Sally Cook
NFL Coach Gene Stalling soul-bearing story of how he struggled to accept and love his son with Down syndrome. New York Times bestseller.

FASTEN YOUR SEATBELT; A CRASH COURSE ON DOWN SYNDROME FOR BROTHERS AND SISTERS
Dr Brian G. Skotko and Susan P. Levine
Dr Skotko, who has a sister with Down syndrome and is a widely respected researcher on Down syndrome pre-natal diagnosis, gives workshops for siblings of children with Down syndrome, and shares his wisdom in this question and answer format book.

CHILDREN'S BOOKS ON DOWN SYNDROME

All are available on Amazon and Barnes and Noble

I CAN, CAN YOU?
Marjorie W. Pitzer author and illustrator
Board book for toddlers depicting young children with Down syndrome and their accomplishments.

BE GOOD TO EDDIE LEE
Virginia Fleming

Three children in the rural South take a walk to the pond and learn a lesson about accepting the uniqueness of Eddie Lee who has Down syndrome.

MY SISTER, ALICIA MAY
Nancy Tupper Ling author
Shennan Bersani illustrator
Beautifully illustrated picture book about two sisters in rural CT, the younger of which, Alicia May has Down syndrome told from the older sister's point of view.

HI, I'M BEN, AND I HAVE DOWN SYNDROME
Julie A Boukamp author
David Tesnar illustrator
Picture book of the daily life of a little boy with Down syndrome.

MY FRIEND HAS DOWN SYNDROME
Jennifer Moore-Mallings author
Marta Fabrega illustrator
Aimed at grade school age children who may be wondering about the differences between them and a classmate with Down syndrome.

VICTORIA'S DAY
Maria de Fatima Campos
Picture book with photos of the daily life of a little girl with Down syndrome.

WHERE IS BEAU?
Suzanne Grinnell author
Joshua Peters illustrator
Second grade reading level book on Kara who has Down syndrome.

OUR BROTHER HAS DOWN'S SYNDROME
Jasmine and Shelley Cairo authors
Irene McNeil illustrator

Book to read to children about Down syndrome illustrated with charming photographs.

My Friend Isabelle
by Eliza Woloson
A little boy describes the differences between himself and his friend Isabelle who has Down syndrome.

BOOKS ON OTHER DISABILITIES

My Child My Gift: A Positive Response to Serious Prenatal Diagnosis
Madeline P. Nugent, Kathy Snow, Mark X Lowney
New City Press
In this collection of stories and practical tips for parents, Nugent reaches out directly to parents who are experiencing a different kind of crisis pregnancy. She gently invites them to consider the experiences of those who have carried children with a serious diagnosis.
www.mychildmygift.com

Precious Treasure: The Story of Patrick
A Place for Me; Patrick's Journey Home
Elizabeth and Mark Matthews, Catholic parents of many children, share their struggle to keep their profoundly autistic son Patrick in their home despite overwhelming challenges. Told with tenderness and deep faith. Elizabeth and Patrick were featured on EWTN's "Life on the Rock".

NOT AVAILABLE ON AMAZON
OR BARNES AND NOBLE

LIFE IS A BLESSING (BIOGRAPHY OF DR JEROME LEJEUNE)
Clara Lejeune Gaymard

Tenderly written story of life with her famous father, Dr Jerome Lejeune. Dr Lejeune discovered trisomy 21 in 1958 and dedicated his life to finding a cure for Down syndrome and testifying to the dignity of life from the tiniest embryo to the disabled. Dr Lejeune's cause for canonization was opened in 2007. Available at the National Catholic Bioethics Center website

Appendix II

Reprints of my articles from the
National Catholic Register.

Down, Not Out
The Legacy of Jerome Lejeune and the
Resurgence of Down Syndrome Research
By Leticia Velasquez, Register Correspondent

There's a battle going on over Down syndrome babies. But these special children also have a patron saint.

Let's look at the battle first.

As if expectant mothers did not have enough to worry about, the American College of Obstetricians and Gynecologists recently recommended that all pregnant women, regardless of age, be screened for Down syndrome.

The college's ethics committee announced in April that it is reconsidering its position. But screening for Down syndrome puts more babies at risk.

Last May, *The New York Times* reported that more than 90% of babies are aborted after a diagnosis of Down syndrome. There are efforts to reverse this trend.

In 2005, while still a student at Harvard, Dr. Brian Skotko, a doctor at Children's Hospital in Boston, released an influential study which exposed the negative attitude of doctors when they inform patients that their baby has Down syndrome.

PRENATALLY AND POSTNATALLY DIAGNOSED CONDITIONS AWARENESS ACT

Reverberations from Skotko's study were felt as far as Capitol Hill.

"Sen. [Sam] Brownback's staffers read about my study in the *Wall Street Journal*," said Skotko, "and, as a result, the 'Prenatally and Postnatally Diagnosed Conditions Awareness Act' was introduced into the Senate."

Defeated in 2005, the bill was reintroduced in 2007 by Sens. Brownback, of Kansas, and [Ted] Kennedy, of Massachusetts. It would provide expectant parents up-to-date, scientifically sound information on the medical treatment available to individuals with Down syndrome, access to support groups for parents and a list of potential adoptive parents.

The bill is awaiting debate in the House, after which there is a good chance it will pass and be signed by President Bush.

Dr. Albert Harris, professor of embryology at the University of North Carolina at Chapel Hill, however, is wary of the bill. His comments that babies with Down syndrome should be aborted ignited a firestorm last February.

Harris explained, "I merely intended to spark debate in my class by playing devil's advocate, and I regret that this misunderstanding inflicted pain upon parents of children with Down syndrome."

While he has expressed a desire to pursue research into a cure for the genetic disorder, he fears that "the bill could have a negative emotional effect upon women who already have chosen termination."

ENCOURAGING RESEARCH DEVELOPMENTS

Promising research at Johns Hopkins Medical School is headed by Dr. Roger Reeves, who said, "I was surprised how successful I was using an agent called SAG [sonic agonist] to help the development of the cerebellum in mice." He is currently investigating the effects of SAG on the hippocampus; both are parts of the brain that are underdeveloped in Down syndrome.

Reeves cited other breakthroughs: "At The Center for Research and Treatment of Down Syndrome at Stanford, Dr. Craig Garner is using DTZ (pentylenetertrazole) to improve the cognitive function of mice, and Dr. Bill Mobley is working to improve the function of synapses between neurons in circuits important for learning and memory."

Mobley stated, "I located a single gene on the 21st chromosome, which is a major contributor to mental impairment and the degeneration of neurons in adults with Down syndrome. There is genuine promise in turning great science into great medicine and Down syndrome is no exception. This field is moving in a terrific direction — one that is bringing new hope for people with Down syndrome."

The Down Syndrome Research and Treatment Foundation fund these programs, which do not use embryonic stem cells.

Recently, the National Institutes of Health drafted a 10-year plan for increasing and coordinating Down syndrome research. Some attribute this modest though encouraging development to the persistence of Down syndrome parent advocacy groups; however, the current federal funding of $17 million is a paltry sum compared to the $128 million allocated to autism research.

These breakthroughs have their medical basis in the work of Dr. Jerome Lejeune, the French geneticist who, in 1958, discovered that Trisomy-21, an extra chromosome on the 21st pair, was responsible for Down syndrome.

Lejeune dedicated his life to finding a cure. As his daughter Clara writes in her memoir, *Life Is a Blessing*, "he believed it would take less work to cure Down syndrome than to travel to the moon."

A Catholic, Lejeune's respect for the sanctity of life continues in the *Fondation Lejeune*, which operates *L'hôpital Saint-Jacques* in Paris for patients with Trisomy-21 and funds 100 research grants to scientists around the world who do research in Down syndrome.

Among them are Dr. Colin McGuckin of Newcastle, England, who discovered the stem cells available in umbilical cord blood, and Dr. Alberto Costa of the University of Colorado who is using memantine, an

FDA-approved drug used to treat Alzheimer's disease, to improve the memory of mice with Trisomy-21.

In the United States, The Michael Fund was formed to further the research of Dr. Lejeune.

Obstetrician and geneticist Dr. Paddy Jim Baggot received a grant in 2004 to pursue biochemical studies on the developing fetal brain. He has just published results of his study of the effects of Vitamin B-2 and B-6 on the fetal brain in *Fetal Diagnosis and Therapy*.

Baggot said, "In the 1970s, when our ability to work with genes was limited, the desire to pursue cures was greater than it is now, when our ability to treat these problems is greater; it is culturally forbidden. There is a pro-abortion mindset which seeks to eliminate those with Down syndrome rather than cure them."

Baggot called on the medical community "to expand their horizons, and find treatments for Down syndrome," which he says, "is the more intelligent thing to do, and would change the culture of the medical profession."

PROTECTOR OF THE 'LITTLE ONES'

Dr. Marie Peeters Ney, who worked with Lejeune for 10 years, describes the importance of his public witness for the sanctity of life: "In the 1960s, at a time when the whole world was falling apart, when heads in the medical community and society in general were swimming with the idea that 'we have the power through pre-natal diagnosis to eradicate disease, as well as those who have the disease,' Dr. Lejeune was the standard-bearer. He stood alone. He stood there long enough so that the next generation could take up the cause. If he had not been there, there would have been nobody."

Pope John Paul II recognized Lejeune's moral courage; the men were close friends and collaborators in fighting the culture of death.

Shortly before Lejeune's death on April 3, 1994, Pope John Paul created the Pontifical Academy for Life, with Lejeune as its first president. Lejeune, deeply honored by this, said, "I'm dying while on special duty."

He left this world saddened by his failure to find the cure for Down syndrome. But there is little doubt that he is still at work, interceding for his "little ones."

On June 28, 2007 the cause for canonization of Jerome Lejeune was introduced, signaling the heroic soul of this pro-life geneticist. Let us hope that his influence will continue to inspire the conscience of the medical profession to serve those with genetic syndromes, and not seek to destroy them.

PRAYER TO OBTAIN GRACES BY GOD'S SERVANT'S INTERCESSION

God, who created man in your image and intended him to share your glory,

We thank you for having granted to your Church the gift of professor Jerome Lejeune, a distinguished servant of life.

He knew how to place his immense intelligence and deep faith at the service of the defense of human life, especially unborn life, always seeking to treat and to cure. A passionate witness to truth and charity, he knew how to reconcile faith and reason in the sight of today's world.

By his intercession, and according to your will, we ask you to grant us the graces we implore, hoping that he will soon become one of your saints. Amen.

As the cause for canonization of Lejeune moves forward, testimonies of medically inexplicable cures sought by his intercession will be recorded, and holy cards with this prayer are available at this address:

Postulation de la cause de beatificación et de canonisation du Serviteur de Dieu Jérôme Lejeune

Abbaye Saint-Wandrille F-76490

Saint-Wandrille, France.

Down, Hero Dad and Palin

By Leticia Velasquez, Register Correspondent

In the wake of the financial debacle where the wiles of Wall Street, with the cooperation of politicians, undermined the economy of this nation, there is a growing cynicism about the possibility of anything worthwhile coming from Congress. Their approval rating is at an all-time low. Enter two farmers, one from Kansas, and another from Virginia. Their confluence of compassion, combined with the star power of one special baby, has resulted in a minor miracle: a unanimous vote in the Senate with the approval of the Prenatally and Postnatally Diagnosed Conditions Awareness Act (S. 1810) on Sept. 23.

I first discussed the bill with Sen. Sam Brownback, R-Kan., at the Blogs for Life Conference at the Family Research Council in January 2007. I had saved an article about his previous sponsorship of this bill, which went down in flames in 2005. It is aimed at parents whose unborn child has been diagnosed with a disability like Down syndrome, spina bifida, cystic fibrosis or other congenital anomalies. This bill would provide the parents with up-to-date information about the prognosis of individuals with this condition, lists of parent support groups, and a registry of potential adoptive parents, should the couple decide not to keep the baby. Currently, the abortion rate for these diagnoses is 90%. When Sen. Brownback heard this statistic, he told me that he had to do something about it. So he joined forces with Sen. Ted Kennedy, D-Mass., whose relatives, the Shrivers, have long supported special-needs initiatives like Best Buddies and Special Olympics.

I was enthusiastic about the bill in the manner of one who is new to business as usual in Washington, believing that this bill would pass on its own merits. I needed to do something to help lower the abortion rate of children with Down syndrome. Since my daughter Christina was born with Down syndrome six years ago, this statistic has haunted me. We parents of children with Down syndrome were incensed in February 2007 when the American College of Obstetricians and Gynecologists recommended universal testing of pregnant women for Down syndrome, and the media felt our ire: *The New York Times* spoke of us as a grassroots movement. But it was not enough to pass the bill, stuck in committee where good ideas so often die. So we spread the news when the bill was reintroduced in Congress in July 2007 to other involved parents — and to pro-life and Catholic periodicals. Along with Down syndrome advocacy organizations, we kept track of the bill's progress.

Suddenly, fate took a stunning turn when Sarah Palin rocketed into the national spotlight this month, her son Trig in her arms. He was a tranquil baby who now put a face on Down syndrome. America was completely smitten by the image of big sister Piper, who, while cradling Trig during her mother's convention speech, licked her hand and smoothed down her little brother's hair. Trig was the focus of affection in America, and again, parents of children with Down syndrome felt our hopes rise: Our bill might be approved.

Sen. Brownback, feeling the energy, took to the floor of the Senate in a bold move to extract his bill from an omnibus one weighted with pork, by requesting a unanimous vote. He had a silent ally: Thomas Vander Woude, a Virginia farmer, devout Catholic, and 66-year-old father of seven. Just a few days before, Tom saw his beloved 20-year-old son Joseph fall into a sewer, where he struggled to breathe, immersed in filth. Without hesitating, Tom dove into the sewer, holding his son's head up so he could be rescued, sacrificing his life for a young man whom 90% of expectant parents reject;

Josie has Down syndrome. Sen. Brownback told Tom's extraordinary story in his speech.

Thomas Vander Woude's mighty expression of fatherly love, combined with Sarah Palin's gentle example of motherly love — refusing to abort a child whose birth complicated her career as governor of Alaska — brought this once forsaken little bill to victory in the Senate.

The power of courageous love had inspired a lackluster, morally bankrupt Senate to a great act — for which it will be long remembered.

Remembering Jerome Lejeune
How a Boy With Down Syndrome
Changed a Geneticist's Career

By LETICIA VELASQUEZ, REGISTER CORRESPONDENT

Clara Lejeune Gaymard has a "servant of God" as a father: Jerome Lejeune, the French geneticist who discovered the cause of Down syndrome.

Lejeune, who died in 1994 at age 67, was outspoken against legal abortion. He was named the first president of the Pontifical Academy for Life shortly before his death by Pope John Paul II.

Life Is a Blessing, A Biography of Jerome Lejeune, by Gaymard, was first published in 1997 in Paris. Subsequently, it was published in English by Ignatius Press — and has just been republished by The National Catholic Bioethics Center.

Register correspondent Leticia Velasquez recently spoke to Gaymard during the "New York Encounter" sponsored by Communion and Liberation.

Why did you decide to write the book?

You know, my father died on Easter 1994, and I was pregnant with my daughter. She was No. 6 and was born 13 days after, and she was like the sunshine coming up after the death of my father. And looking at this little girl, I was thinking, She will never know her grandfather, so I have to write for her.

So I started to write the story of my father ... because it was sad that he was dead, but all the good memories we had with him were good: He was a funny guy; he was always giving a lot of love, and so I wanted her to know about him. And, during the summer, I showed what I wrote to a journalist, and he told me, "You should make a book," and this is the story of the book. It's the story, only the very simple story, of a daughter who loves her father and wants to remember.

The love you have for your father is quite evident in the book; it brings him out as a family man as well as a scientist. What was the effect of this book? Do you think it had any effect on his cause for canonization?

I wouldn't pretend that. What is very important for us is that, when he was alive, he took care of children with Down syndrome; he had a consultation with more than 5,000 patients, and he knew them, each of them, by the first name. The day before he died, I met him at the hospital, and he said to me, "You know, I'm not afraid to leave, but I'm sad for my patients, because they won't understand why I should be the one who tried to save them, and I abandoned them." So I told him, "You know they will understand; they understand better than we do." And he told me, "No, they don't understand better than we do, but deeper."

So, when I came back home with my sister, my brother and my mom, we said, "We have to continue his work." So we decided to create, at first, an association, and then a foundation, so we could cure the children and put as much money as we could to continue the research that he wanted to do.

So, that is the purpose of Foundation Lejeune – you do medical research, funding, and you also have a clinic?

Yes, we have a clinic, and we have a lot of Down syndrome children in Europe, so there are a lot of new patients who are coming in. But the eldest is 72, so we have a large range of patients coming. Some are doing fine; some are sick. The purpose is that my father was convinced that there is a strong connection between research and clinic, and they find that in many systems you become a researcher and you forget the clinic, and it's a big mistake, and he wanted to keep the relationship between clinical practice and research. So it's what we have done in the foundation, the consultation, so that you can observe the patient and help them and also finance and do the research.

You yourself do not work full time for the foundation.

No, I'm not working for the foundation. I'm the daughter; I'm not a scientist or a physician, so you have to leave the real one to do the job. So, I'm a member of the foundation, but I'm working for General Electric. I'm the CEO for France, and I'm working for the international level, to develop the connection of GE with government and cities. So, I have an international job, and I'm the mother of nine children.

What are the speeches that you are giving in New York today [Jan. 15]?

You know, this is a kind of miracle. We thought that it was a good idea to create a foundation here in the U.S., because we are giving quite a lot of money to scientists here: We have already financed 61 projects, and 30 teams in the U.S., so we felt it was the right time to start something here. The "New York Encounter" team contacted us and said it would be a good time for me to speak about my father. I hope that today we will remember in a couple of years that it was the day that the Foundation Jerome Lejeune started in the U.S.

Tell me about your family.

My husband is a politician. He has been minister ... of health, minister of economy and finance and minister of agriculture too. Now he is head of a region in France, and he's also a member of Parliament. He's traveling a lot in France, and I'm traveling abroad, so we joke about it. Our children live in Paris. They are between 23 and 12; they are very close, so we are really a team. They do very diverse things: One is a publisher; one is a journalist; one studies archeology; one is working in movies and cinema; one is an artist, and she sings; and the other is in political science, and the three youngest are still in school.

Since your book is being republished, have you ever considered giving movie rights to, let's say, a Catholic movie company to do a biopic?

Ahhh, I would love to, if someone asked me.

I believe it's a story made for a movie.

Yes, I think it is, because, you know, my father, he was a gifted man — really, he was very clever, and he was very handsome. He was the kind of man you love. You know, I'm traveling all the time — I'm in economics and business — and every time I am traveling, I meet someone who has met my father. He was the kind of guy that, when you meet him once, you would never forget him. And he had a beautiful career. He was a scientist; he made a big discovery; he became the first geneticist in France, very young, the top of the newspapers, advisor to the president; and one day, he decided, "I cannot accept abortion," not because he is Christian, but because he knows as a geneticist that life starts at conception. And he had to say it. He had to protect the ones whom they want to kill, who are too young to protect themselves.

So he started this fight as a scientist, saying, "I have to tell the truth. I'm not judging anyone; I'm not saying anything else besides the truth of the science, and I have to testify about that."

Do you remember that when you were growing up?

I remember it so clearly. I was 10 years old, and, one day, he came home for lunch. The day before, on television, there was a movie about a family where a woman had a child with Down syndrome, and she wanted to abort, and she couldn't do it then.

After, there was a debate about abortion of the diseased children, and a boy came to his consultation with his mom, and he was crying, and my father said, "Why are you crying?" And his mother said, "He saw the movie, and I couldn't stop him crying," and then he jumped in my father's arms, and he was only 10 with Down syndrome. He said, "You know, they want to kill us. And you have to save us, because we are too weak, and we can't do anything." And [my father] came back home for lunch, and he was white, and he said, "If I don't protect them, I am nothing." That's how it started.

And then his career came down. He didn't have money for his research. He was like a pariah, and so on, but he accepted that because he thought he was doing that which was his duty.

But it affected you as children as well. You were very fearful, no?

I wouldn't use that word. He never put it as a drama. He didn't say, "It's terrible." Mama was very supportive of him, the fact that we had a father who only said what science said. Okay, he had a lot of critics, people who were blaming him and saying horrible things about him, but since we knew him and that he was just doing what he had to do, we had a respect and love for him. We accepted the fact that we were also pariahs at school. But we took it like we were a very normal family.

So, you never resented the extra suffering that it might have caused the family?

I had a lot of obstacles to some jobs and, very recently, four years ago, I was going to have a very important job, and the CEO wanted me to have the job, but the president said, "I can't accept her because she is the daughter of this man." And so the CEO asked her to meet me, and she did and said, "She is wonderful, but I can't accept her." So the CEO said, "It's like racism." And she admitted, "Yes, but I can't accept her; it's impossible." She thought I was perfect, but you know, I was the daughter.

That kind of thing doesn't happen much anymore, but it's because it wasn't my place. I have a very nice position here as well. I am very happy in GE, so that's good.

What do you hope will happen as a result of your book being republished?

First of all, I am very grateful to the people who took so much energy and courage to publish it again. I hope that, first of all, it would give hope to people, because this book is the story of a family. And what has happened since I published this book in France is that I received about 2,000 letters. One woman told me she read the book to a blind priest who was going to die and wanted this book to be read before he died. Another woman wanted to tell me the story she had with her father. Another time, it was a young girl of 15 who said, "I want to do the same job as your father."

It can speak to the hearts of the people who read it, and they feel that, in many cases, they have lived the same things, because, hopefully, in most of the families, parents love the children, the children love the parents, so that the book is just the story of a normal life — so they can be reminded of the good and bad times they had, the sense of humanity which is starting with the family. If they can raise their heads and say, "I'm not alone; everything is possible — and I can do it."

Are there any recorded miracles from people who have prayed for your father's intercession?

Many people are saying that praying to him has changed their lives, but we don't have any medical miracles yet.

These articles are reprinted with permission from the *National Catholic Register.*

Acknowledgements

When I first began sharing my stories about Christina in 2006, and was discouraged that medical professionals were not willing to share them with their patients whose child was prenatally diagnosed, I began my blogs Causa Nostrae Laetitiae and Cause of Our Joy.

The first time I ventured beyond my blogs, I sent stories to Monica Rafie at *Be Not Afraid* and Mary Kellett at *Prenatal Partners for Life*. It was at these sites I found kindred spirits, and encouragement for this project. Monica Rafie found many of the stories in this book, encouraged me in my writing, and helped me write queries to publish this book. Heidi Hess Saxton gave me my first major article in *Canticle* magazine; "Pro-life in the Public Square; Catholic Politicians Who Stood their Ground" which gave me the courage to interview politicians. The politician most Catholics wanted to name as a Catholic hero for that story was former Senator Rick Santorum who kindly allowed me to reprint an article on his daughter Bella for this book, making us a special mom *and* dad's book. Without such gifted contributors I could never have accomplished what God has called me to do in this book; encourage the frightened parent who feels he or she is unequal to the call to special parenting.

For my family who has had less elegant dinners thanks to my three years of work on this book, thank you for your help, your input and most of all, your belief that someday, this book would make it to print. To my daughter Gabbi who shared my excitement, helped me stay focused and did a lot of clean up work on the book, thank you. To Michele Merrinan Berg a professional editor and aunt to two special needs children whose countless hours of volunteer editing made this book as polished as it is. To Sandra Cloutier who formatted the photos optimizing the beauty of our children, thank you. To my talented friends Sherry Boas and Tina

Dennelly, who did final editing, thank you. For my mother Eleanor, now with God, who always knew I was called to write and never let me forget it. Thank you.

For Servant of God, Dr Jerome Lejeune, who I know is interceding for those with Down syndrome and other disabilities from Heaven, *merci mon bon professeur!*

Epilogue

**Some advice from Fr Frank Pavone, National
Director of Priests for Life**

I would like to give the last lines of this book to a priest whose name has become synonymous with the culture of life: Fr Frank Pavone. His heroic action to save Baby Joseph Maarachli was a lesson to the world that the lives of our special needs children are priceless, no matter how long God gives them to us.

In the early hours of Holy Thursday, 2011, as Churches were preparing – and in some parts of the world already celebrating – the Mass of the Lord's Supper and the washing of the feet, "Baby Joseph" was flown from St Louis, where he has been treated since I brought him there in mid-March, to his home in Windsor, Canada. As the Church prepared to celebrate the day when the Lord gave us the command to "love one another," Baby Joseph's parents and older brother were enjoying the fruit of the hard fight that their love inspired. They fought to help their baby breathe and bring him home. Canadian medical and government authorities had resisted, trying to impose their own value judgment on his life.

Now, however, he was home, and the Priests for Life Family, including tens of thousands of people who sent emails to the Canadian authorities, is delighted to have helped.

Our mission to save Baby Joseph and help his family was never based on any prediction of the future, but rather on the value of his life here and now. Our critics, on the other hand, looking into the crystal ball that 'right to die' advocates seem to always think they have, claimed our intervention was futile because Joseph would only end up having a machine do his breathing for him.

We don't have to answer their criticism; Joseph is doing that for us, with every breath he takes. He has gained benefit from his tracheotomy, is breathing on his own, and is free from the need to use any tubes or machines.

Doctors have not given a time estimate as to how long they think he will live. Nobody knows. What we do know is that there are several key lessons to draw from this story:

a) **Doctors do not always know best.** Day by day, situations turn out better than many doctors predict. The desires of the patient and the family who seek care need to be honored.

b) **Families need to fight to care for their loved ones.** Moe Maraachli and his wife Sana did just that. They did not let the death of a previous child bring them to despair about this one. Rather, they fought hard for Joseph to get the care that has now helped him. Their love reminded me of the love that Terri Schiavo's parents and siblings showed for her, a love willing to persevere despite the public spotlight and pressure that they never sought.

c) **The meaning and value of life does not come from medical tribunals or courts, and it is not measured in years, months, or days.** It is measured by giving and receiving love, first from God and then from each other.

d) **When people band together for the cause of life, victories can be won.** So many people sent emails, prayed, and are helping pay for Baby Joseph's care (see **BabyJosephCentral. com**). We need to stay engaged in the pro-life cause, because there are many more victories to win.